What People Are Saying About Women in Law

"*Women in Law Discovering the True Meaning of Success* is an insightful book and a must-read for any woman lawyer who is either at the beginning of her career or thinking about transitioning from her current job. With candor, compassion, and humor, the authors address how they overcame self-doubt, mistakes, and impostor syndrome to chart their own unique professional journeys, fueled by a passion for their work and their desire to help other women advance and succeed. Their inspiring real-life stories vividly demonstrate the importance of mentors, sponsors, family, and friends, and even an online sisterhood of advisors. The many concrete strategies, tips, and advice they impart will help you define your own meaning of success on your terms, rather than what others may expect of you. This book is an indispensable guide to help you navigate through any challenge or obstacle you may encounter during your career."

—*Roberta "Bobbi" Liebenberg*, former Chair, ABA Commission on Women in the Profession; Principal, The Red Bee Group; and Senior Partner, Fine, Kaplan and Black

"[*Women in Law*] is an important and very readable book. Being a woman lawyer is given so many different nuances by the various contributors, showing that everyone's journey is different. It comes across clearly that there are so many different paths to success and what 'success' means will be different for each woman. What success means will also change as life changes. This is one of the key themes in the book—that the conventional notion of a 'successful lawyer' may not be what actually brings you personal success. Many of the women featured achieved amazing successes but then questioned how fulfilling those successes actually were for them, and they were able to move in new directions. There's an important message for the legal profession: We need to consistently question what 'success' looks like and if it is out of reach of some because of definitions that are too narrow and now outdated. This is a book about women who are lawyers; but its message is important for all lawyers and even for all professionals working during this time when how we work and why we work is changing."

—*Dr. Catherine McGregor MCMI ChMC*, Management Consultant and author of *Business Thinking in Practice for In-house Counsel*

"The authors of *Women in Law Discovering the True Meaning of Success* know the power of stories, and this book is chock full of illuminating and inspiring ones. The rich, diverse voices of women attorneys beckon the reader to reflect on the many experiences shared, and then seem to invite the reader to write their own unique story—to say, 'I dare you not to.'"

—*Michele Mayes*, General Counsel, New York Public Library; co-author, *Courageous Counsel: Conversations with Women General Counsel in the Fortune 500*; and former Chair, ABA Commission on Women in the Profession

"*Women in Law: Discovering the True Meaning of Success* provides the answer to anyone who wants to go to law school but hesitates out of fear, lack of confidence, or ill-considered advice. There are countless ways to use the skills that accompany a legal education. The stories in this book demonstrate that you can create your own definition of success. As these women share, the first step is to silence your fears."

—*Lauren Stiller Rikleen*, President, Rikleen Institute for Strategic Leadership, and author of *The Shield of Silence: How Power Perpetuates a Culture of Harassment and Bullying in the Workplace* and *You Raised Us, Now Work With Us: Millennials, Career Success, and Building Strong Workplace Teams*

WOMEN IN LAW

DISCOVERING
THE TRUE MEANING
OF SUCCESS

An Anthology

WOMEN IN LAW

Discovering the True Meaning of Success

AUTHORS

Michelle Banks

Bellina Barrow

Jennifer Belmont Jennings

Jenn Deal

Rebecca Evans

Bhavna Fatnani

Pat Gillette

Zeynep Goral

Tatia Gordon-Troy

Angela Han

Talar Herculian Coursey

Marta Keller

Elena Kohn

Maja Larson

Nhu-Y Le

Krista Lynn

Lisa Quinn O'Flaherty

Christine Payne

Suzie Smith

Jamie Sternberg

Heather Stevenson

Jamie Szal

Lauren Tetenbaum

EDITOR

Tatia Gordon-Troy

RAMSES HOUSE PUBLISHING LLC
BALTIMORE, MD

Published by Ramses House Publishing LLC, Baltimore, MD
www.publishingforlawyers.com
First Printing, 2022
ISBN 979-8-9855653-0-0 paperback

Notice: The book is written for prelaw students, law students, and new attorneys. Its purpose is to educate women in the legal field on how to define their own professional success.

Library of Congress Control Number: 2022902481
Printed and bound in the United States of America

The cover image is used under license from Shutterstock

Contents

Feel free to follow or connect with the authors on LinkedIn

About the Authors

Feel free to follow or connect with the authors on LinkedIn

MICHELLE BANKS is a Senior Advisor at BarkerGilmore specializing in providing executive coaching to corporate general counsel. She also leads law department strategic retreats and professional development workshops. Michelle is co-founder of UCLA Law Women LEAD, a network of more than 3,000 women law students and alumnae at her alma mater, where she also guest teaches annually in the professional development program.

Michelle serves as a member of the board of directors of DirectWomen, a nonprofit whose mission is to prepare women lawyers to serve on the boards of directors of major companies. She also sits on the women's leadership board at Orrick law firm, annually chairs the Ms. JD LaddHer Up retreat, and is a frequent speaker on leadership. Until 2016, Michelle was Executive Vice President, Global General Counsel, Corporate Secretary, and Chief Compliance Officer of global apparel retailer Gap Inc.

Before joining Gap Inc. in 1999, Michelle worked as legal counsel for the Golden State Warriors NBA team and in Tokyo as American counsel for Itochu Corporation. Her prior law firm practice with Sheppard Mullin and Morrison & Foerster in California and New York focused on corporate finance and international commercial transactions.

Michelle has been recognized locally and nationally for her professional accomplishments and her dedication to enhancing the careers of others, including as a Legend in Law by the Burton Foundation, a Distinguished General Counsel by the Directors

Roundtable, a Top General Counsel to Watch by *Corporate Board Member,* a Corporate Counsel Innovator by the *Financial Times,* an Influential Woman in Bay Area Business and a Corporate Counsel Diversity Champion by the *San Francisco Business Times,* a Most Powerful and Influential Woman by California Diversity Council, and a Woman of Achievement by Legal Momentum.

Santa Clara University Law School presented Michelle with its Social Justice and Human Rights award in 2014 and UCLA Law School named her 2016 Alumni of the Year for Professional Achievement. In 2019, Michelle received the American Bar Association's Margaret Brent Woman Lawyer of Achievement award— the highest honor bestowed on a woman lawyer by the ABA.

BELLINA BARROW, a Trinidad & Tobago national, is an independent legal practitioner with a prior career in human resources. She was admitted to legal practice in Trinidad & Tobago in 2012 and in Antigua & Barbuda in 2014. She has experience in labour/employment law, administrative/public law, real property compulsory acquisition, personal injury, insurance, trust, and contract law matters.

While Bellina has represented clients in various sectors, she has particular experience in aviation, insurance, trust, financial services, tourism, and telecommunications sectors. She is a legal author and a former national table tennis player with interests in playing and spectating sports, travelling, reading, current affairs, and technology.

JENNIFER BELMONT JENNINGS, JD, CFP® is a Wealth Advisor at Hightower Wealth Advisors| St. Louis, where she works with individuals and families to build a legacy by developing and implementing financial plans that complement their estate planning and tax objectives. Earlier in her career, Jennifer practiced law focusing on estate planning, probate, and family matters, which provides her with perspective and experience to act as a bridge between the financial and legal aspects of her clients' lives.

Jennifer received her JD, MA, and BA from Washington University in St. Louis, and completed the General Course Program at The London School of Economics and Political Science (LSE). She is a committed community volunteer and serves on the board of directors for several local nonprofits. Jennifer was also recognized by the *St. Louis Business Journal* as a "40 Under 40" in 2020.

Jennifer, her husband, Brent, and their son, Liam, live in St. Louis. In addition to family volunteer activities, they enjoy golf and traveling. Connect with Jennifer on Instagram *@money.tea.legacy.*

JENN DEAL is a life coach and a lawyer. As a life coach, Jenn coaches high-achieving women who feel stuck and unfulfilled despite being successful by all objective standards. These are women who have worked hard to get where they are but don't feel like it's ever enough. Jenn helps women ditch the perfectionism, people pleasing, overwhelm, and self-judgment that is holding them back and create the big, bold, satisfying lives they know they were meant to live. Visit www.jenndealcoaching.com.

As a lawyer, Jenn specializes in complex and contentious trademark and trade dress infringement, false advertising, and unfair competition matters.

REBECCA EVANS is known by her clients as a "friend." The attorneys who fight her call her "sophisticated" and "terrifying." She is passionate about helping her clients get fair results and increasing their access to justice. She's a legal maverick and entrepreneur who has run several small businesses successfully and knows what it takes to keep the lights on and provide for a family.

Rebecca gained fame as the attorney who simultaneously sued nine state bars to remove the last remaining unconstitutional restrictions on business names for law firms. Her team won all nine suits. She also filed the biggest mass tort case in history against GoSmith for telemarketing spam, putting her clients' privacy back in their own hands.

Rebecca most recently served as Chief Legal Officer and Managing Partner of LawHQ for two years before opening Evans Law to focus on small business owners and families.

Rebecca loves to bake, hike, and travel and is just learning how to ski after a rocky start. She has six children (they all ski better than she does!), two dogs, and a wonderful husband who can often be found mountain biking or in the kitchen cooking and singing off-key.

BHAVNA FATNANI is a licensed lawyer and Company Secretary from India with six years of experience in legal research, drafting, and providing cost-effective compliance solutions. Her expertise includes matters of corporate and commercial laws. She is currently associated with Ernst & Young where her role encompasses aspects of contract management and compliances for anti-money laundering laws and policies.

Being passionate about writing, Bhavna actively engages with the writers' community and takes up projects as a freelancer. Her articles have been published and acclaimed in *ReportHER* (India's first women's only newspaper) since 2017. She also has contributed as a guest author. Bhavna has taken the first step in personal branding and is engaging using the personal hashtag #HerstorieswithBhavna on social media.

While keeping up with work and her passion for writing, Bhavna believes in giving back to society. For this, she offers mentorship about law, advice on the NCA accreditation process, and shares her journey as an immigrant (PR holder) in Canada. She has been a guest speaker for podcasts (A Shot of Life and Budding Lawyers) where she shared her experiences as an NCA candidate.

Staying put during the pandemic, Bhavna decided to help the community. She is a Council Member of WICCI Maharashtra Wellness & Wellbeing Council [2020–21] where she actively contributes her creative thoughts for designing and content creation with an aim to impact 10,000 women in Maharashtra, empowering and educating them to grow in different facets of life. Bhavna also hosted two live interactions during the series "Re-invent Yourself" in June 2021 covering how to elevate your career and how to be an effective entrepreneur.

Visit Bhavna's website at www.ibhavna.com.

P AT GILLETTE is one of the country's leading experts and most sought-after speakers on gender diversity and equality. Rated as a top employment litigator and trial lawyer by Chambers and other organizations for 40 years and as a leader and rainmaker in her firms, Pat's legal career focused on assisting Fortune 500 companies with their most difficult issues and challenges. At the end of 2015, she resigned from her firm to pursue her passion for empowering women through keynote speaking and writing. She now tours the country speaking on issues that help women advance into leadership positions in their organizations. Pat was invited to join JAMS in 2016 and now spends some of her time mediating employment cases.

Pat has been recognized for her work to advance women in the legal profession by many organizations. She is the 2018 recipient of the ABA Margaret Brent award, the highest honor given to women lawyers for professional achievement and for advancing the interests of women lawyers. She also has received the ABA Golden Hammer award, the California Women Lawyers Association's Fay Stender award, the Transformational Leadership award as one of the Top Women Rainmakers, and the Barristers Association of San Francisco Award of Merit.

Pat is the Co-Founder of the Opt-In Project, a nationwide initiative focused on changing the structure of law firms to increase the retention and advancement of women. The team she co-chaired at the 2016 Hackathon created the Mansfield Rule, which has now been adopted by several law firms and corporations across the country as a means of immediately impacting the opportunities for women to advance into leadership positions.

Pat has been a commissioner on the ABA Commission on Women in the Profession, a member of ABA's Gender Equity Task Force, co-chair of the BASF No Glass Ceiling Initiative, and has served on several nonprofit boards dedicated to protecting and promoting women. She is currently a board member of DirectWomen and Girls Leadership.

Pat's newest book, *Rainmakers: Born or Bred*, is filled with practical tactics and strategies that can be easily implemented to enhance business development skills and expand books of business. In the book, she highlights the nationally acclaimed Rainmaker Study and includes helpful tips from rainmakers and clients across the country.

Pat is the proud mother of two successful and enlightened sons and lives in Kensington, CA, with her husband of 40-plus years. She has served as an elected official of her town and is active in political and community organizations and activities.

Visit www.patriciagillette.com or contact her at 510.604.6252.

ZEYNEP GORAL is a trilingual attorney turned legal content copywriter who also publishes fiction under a pen name. She graduated *magna cum laude* from Boston University with a double major in international relations and Japanese language and literature. She graduated law school from the University of Pennsylvania in 2010 and lived in Philadelphia for a few years until she packed up her dog and moved to Los Angeles.

Zeynep took an interest in web design when she was 14 and taught herself to code. She worked for several years as an attorney in Los Angeles before committing fulltime to her legal copywriting and marketing business. Visit www.zgcreativeagency.com.

Zeynep was born in Istanbul, Turkey, and moved to Nashville, TN, with her parents at the age of 6. She currently lives in Los Angeles with her soft-coated wheaten terrier, Sophie.

TATIA GORDON-TROY uses the hashtag #behindthebook because she has been the brains behind hundreds of books written by attorneys during her 30-year career as an editor, writer, and publisher. As the former head of publishing for the American Immigration Lawyers Association where she was successful at building a multi-million-dollar publishing house, Tatia was instrumental in transforming many attorneys into successful authors and thought leaders. Tatia is a Maryland attorney, an experienced journalist, and an award-winning editor who is passionate about good writing and making people sound better than they ever thought they could. What author wouldn't want that?

As the CEO of Ramses House Publishing LLC, a publishing consultancy and author services company, Tatia serves as a writing coach, a developmental and structural editor, an author educator, a ghostwriter, and an all-around miracle worker. She continues to work with attorneys and other professionals to independently publish their work and leverage their expertise to better market themselves and their practices while attracting high-end clientele. She also works closely with small associations to teach them how to strategically use content to build non-dues revenue and to repurpose, reuse, and recycle content to increase member outreach. Visit her website at www.publishingforlawyers.com.

Tatia regularly speaks on topics including content marketing, thought leadership, publishing, branding, and social media. Her articles have appeared on AttorneyAtWork.com and in *Attorney at Law* magazine and the *Maryland Bar Journal*. She is a member of the Maryland Bar Association and serves on the Associations Council of the Association Media & Publishing Network.

Tatia graduated *summa cum laude* from Morgan State University with a business degree and received her JD from the University of Baltimore School of Law. In her spare time, she loves to travel. She shares her home with her 20-year-old son who is in college and a cat named Kat.

ANGELA HAN is an attorney, life coach, and host of the Fit to Practice podcast. She is Senior Corporate Counsel at HealthPRO Heritage, where she handles commercial transactions, corporate litigation, and labor and employment matters. As a life coach for lawyers, she works with lawyers around the world on getting unstuck and out of indecision.

Angela graduated from Northwestern University with a degree in social policy and graduated from Georgetown University Law Center. She also has a master's in elementary education and teaching from the University of Nevada.

Angela has been hosting the Fit to Practice podcast where she interviews lawyers about their personal and professional journey and what it means to be fit to practice law. She is a certified yoga teacher and former personal trainer with a certification in precision nutrition.

Angela is a fan of Game of Thrones and lives in Ellicott City, MD, with her husband, children, and two cats.

TALAR HERCULIAN COURSEY is a lawyer by day and a philanthropist by night. Talar has served as General Counsel for Vista Ford Lincoln in Woodland Hills and Oxnard, CA, since 2011. Before that, she was a file clerk, associate, and partner at the national labor and employment law firm, Fisher Phillips LLP.

Talar is a co-author of the Amazon bestselling anthology, *#Networked*, and author of a children's book, *Ralphy's Rules for Living the Good Life*, both of which are available on Amazon (all profits going to charities).

Talar has served as the president of the Salt Lake City Chapter for the Society for Orphaned Armenian Relief (SOAR) since 2015. SOAR, founded in 2005, supports orphanages in Syria, Lebanon, and Armenia. To date, Talar has raised over $50,000 for the orphanages in Lebanon in memory of her father, Mardig Herculian. Talar's philanthropy motivated her to write *Ralphy's Rules for Living the Good Life* to raise money for SOAR.

In addition to being a mother, wife, lawyer, and philanthropist, Talar is also a runner and a yogi. She is a self-proclaimed Jesus, Ekhart Tolle, Brené Brown, Glennon Doyle, and Brandon Flowers groupie.

MARTA KELLER is on a mission to help female lawyers go from feeling as if they're not enough and stressed out all the time to feeling happy and having more work-life balance and fulfillment so they can live their own version of success—within or outside the law—without burning out or ending up with vicarious trauma. Using practical and simple body-based tools that can be practiced anywhere without anyone noticing, she helps lawyers understand and partner with their bodies to heal at the nervous system level.

Marta is most excited to work with women who have been feeling stuck or lost in their lives and careers despite seeking help in talk therapy, peer groups, meditation, yoga, breathwork, etc. She helps lawyers who've had a traumatic experience practicing law or who work with emotionally charged or traumatized clients go from overwhelmed, exhausted, and stressed out to experiencing more confidence, peace, and ease so that they can have a rewarding career in or outside of the law—without burning out or ending up with vicarious trauma.

Marta is a former lawyer, having practiced in both civil litigation and indigenous reconciliation for five years. She witnessed the devastating effects of trauma in her work with sexual abuse survivors. She also personally experienced the overwhelming effects of vicarious trauma after choosing to push through feeling unwell instead of listening to the messages of support her body was sending her.

Marta is completing her coaching certification in Organic Intelligence®—an embodied, integrated, and natural approach to bringing stability to the nervous system so that true healing and long-lasting growth and change can happen. She offers one-on-one and group coaching as well as a corporate training program in wellbeing and resilience.

ELENA KOHN serves as Vice President, Associate General Counsel for Women's Care, a national Ob-Gyn group with practices in Florida, California, and Kentucky. Women's Care delivers every 10th baby in the entire state of Florida annually.

As experienced in-house counsel, Elena works closely with the business team as a trusted partner, tailoring legal advice to the specifics of the company. The focus of her legal career is on where business and health/corporate/employment laws meet. At Women's Care, Elena is responsible for operational legal guidance in Florida and Kentucky.

Prior to Women's Care, Elena served as General Counsel for Alliance PTP, a premier national provider of physical therapy services, and also as General Counsel for Dental Partners, which is a national dental services organization that consolidated practices through its integrated delivery systems. Elena was also in-house legal counsel for DaVita Medical Group. While at DaVita, she offered business teammates legal advice in healthcare law and general corporate law.

Before moving in-house, Elena was an associate attorney with the healthcare and corporate practice groups at Shumaker, an Am Law 200 firm where her primary focus was on advising physicians and hospitals on regulatory issues and entity formation and assisting with healthcare-related mergers and acquisitions.

Elena graduated with distinction from University College London in England and graduated *cum laude* from Stetson University College of Law in St. Petersburg, FL. During her law school years, she interned for two federal judges—Judge Elizabeth Kovachevich, U.S. District Judge for the Middle District of Florida, and Judge Thomas Wilson, U.S. Magistrate Judge for the Middle District of Florida. She was also a member of Stetson Law's award-winning Moot Court Board, becoming a finalist at Willem C. Vis international commercial arbitration competition in Vienna, Austria. At her law school graduation, Elena was the recipient of the Walter Mann award in recognition of having shown the greatest promise of becoming an outstanding leader in the legal profession as determined by both faculty and student body. This award is only given to one graduating student per year.

As for hobbies, Elena is an avid Peloton rider (leaderboard name #Law_Mama_Saurus). She is a passionate advocate for cancer research and walked 60 miles in three days to collect funds for Susan G. Komen for the Cure and placed third in a 5K run for Celma Mastry Ovarian Cancer Foundation. Elena has two children and loves fine-tuning her debate skills with her young daughter. For an extra challenge, she takes on her teenage son—and sometimes wins.

MAJA LARSON is Vice President, Client Services, for Equinox Business Law Group PLLC, a boutique law firm providing general counsel solutions tailored to small and mid-sized businesses. She is responsible for the delivery of client services and professional development of the attorney team. She is also an adjunct law professor at Seattle University School of Law, teaching practical in-house counsel skills.

For over 20 years, Maja has advised executives and board members at public and private technology and biotechnology companies and nonprofit corporations with a focus on making strategic decisions based on risk appetite. She created MDL Consulting PLLC, a firm focused on supporting growing technology companies and nonprofits with enterprise risk, board governance, and legal management matters after leaving her position as Vice President, General Counsel and Corporate Secretary of the Allen Institute, a nonprofit medical research organization.

At the Allen Institute, Maja built and matured the legal, corporate governance, technology transfer, enterprise risk, crisis management, grants management, and research compliance functions. Prior to that, Maja was Vice President and Associate General Counsel at Expedia, Inc. with a portfolio including corporate, securities, and M&A matters, and significant commercial contracting and strategic business advice.

Maja started her career as a lawyer at Preston, Gates & Ellis (now K&L Gates) where she worked primarily on corporate and securities transactions and was on the team representing Expedia in its IPO. In her first career chapter, Maja managed legal matters at a publicly traded shipyard, managed franchisees at a publicly traded pizza company, and learned SEC reporting in the finance department of a waterjet manufacturing company.

She is currently serving on advisory boards for two legal startup companies; is a member of the Board of Trustees of the Museum of History and Industry (MOHAI); is on the Board of Bar Examiners for the Washington State Bar Association; and is an angel investor and advisor for startups. Maja holds a JD from Seattle University School of Law and a BA from the University of Washington.

NHU-Y LE is Vice President, Client Services, at Legalpad, an immigration legal tech startup, where she leads a large team of lawyers. She was previously in-house counsel at a Fortune 100 technology company. Nhu-Y graduated from Boston College Law School. In her free time, she likes to watch cooking shows and read murder mystery novels. Follow her for U.S. immigration updates on LinkedIn.

KRISTA LYNN currently serves as Deputy General Counsel of Airbus-OneWeb Satellites on the space coast of Florida. She is licensed to practice law in NY, NJ, DC, PA, and FL, and is admitted to the bar of the U.S. Supreme Court. Throughout her years of practice, Krista has counseled businesses ranging from startups to Fortune 50 companies.

Krista is an entrepreneur and blogger. She is the founder of General Counsel U, a membership community for law students, associates wanting to make the transition to in-house, and current in-house counsel looking to level up their careers. She is also the founder of "Recovering Superwoman," a blog and safe space created to encourage and normalize vulnerability among working professionals.

Most importantly, Krista is a full-time single mom to Nico (5), Gabriella (3), and Milana (2).

CHRISTINE PAYNE is a nationally recognized, Chambers-ranked advocate specializing in eDiscovery and litigation strategy. Christine handles all aspects of case strategy and discovery for complex commercial litigation, restructuring-related litigation, products liability litigation, Section 220 requests, antitrust matters, and ongoing or anticipated investigations. Christine also teaches, speaks, and writes frequently about eDiscovery strategy and advocacy.

Christine is on the board of the Boys & Girls Club of the Austin Area in Texas, which serves the community by providing a safe space for kids to learn, play, and grow. She has three dogs and a mess of chickens and is the mom of two very cool kids, Ty and Addie.

LISA QUINN O'FLAHERTY is a partner in the Irish law firm, Fitzsimons Redmond. She is qualified as a solicitor in Ireland, as well as in England, Wales, and Northern Ireland. She holds an LLB in Irish Law as well as a Professional Diploma in Leadership and Certificates in Media, Technology Law, and Data Protection.

Lisa is currently studying for a Professional Diploma in International Arbitration. She is a trustee to a mental health charity in her spare time and sits on the boards of a number of community organisations. She lives in Dublin with her wonderful husband and two fantastic boys.

SUZIE SMITH started her education at Ivy Tech with an associate's degree in paralegal studies and received her bachelor's from Liberty University in 2015. She received her JD in 2017 from Indiana University Robert H. McKinney School of Law. Since 2017, she has been admitted to the Indiana bar and is admitted to practice before the U.S. District Court for the Northern and Southern Districts of Indiana. Suzie is a member of the American Bar Association, Indiana State Bar Association, Indianapolis Bar Association, and Montgomery County Bar Association.

Suzie's devotion to her community reflects in her serving with the Animal Welfare board and the Crisis Shelter board. She is also active in Women in Networking and Indiana Federation of Business and Professional Women.

Suzie is married to Gary Smith and they live outside of Ladoga with their five daughters—Adriana, Heaven, Paige, Blessing, and Hope. She spends her free time with her family, watching her girls swim in their pond. The girls are avid swimmers and they are on the swim team at Southmont. Suzie also enjoys fitness and being outdoors with her family. As a family, they enjoy reading and visiting the various libraries in Montgomery County.

JAMIE STERNBERG is Counsel with Saunders & Silverstein LLP, a leading trademark and copyright law firm trusted by some of the most well-known brands in the world. Jamie has passionately worked in the field of trademark and copyright law since 2005. She has worked with companies with one trademark to those with worldwide portfolios that include famous trademarks.

Jamie's practice focuses on strategic counseling, prosecution, enforcement, and transactions with respect to trademarks, copyrights, and domain names. Jamie advises clients on obtaining and maintaining domestic and foreign trademark protection. She has successfully registered hundreds of trademarks with the U.S. Patent and Trademark Office. In addition, she advises clients on the availability of new trademarks for use and registration, and develops strategies to protect and enforce intellectual property assets worldwide.

Jamie routinely enforces trademarks and copyrighted material on the internet, including taking down infringing domain names and content on websites, mobile applications, and social media platforms. Jamie also litigates opposition and cancellation actions before the Trademark Trial and Appeal Board.

Jamie has been recognized as a top trademark attorney in the 2021 edition of *World Trademark Review* "WTR 1000" and is ranked among World IP Forum's 2021 list of 250 Powerful Women in IP. Jamie has been a member of the International Trademark Association since 2014 and currently serves on the Famous and Well-Known Marks Committee.

Jamie routinely speaks on trademark and copyright issues and uses LinkedIn as a creative outlet and tool to educate professionals about topics in the world of trademarks and business development. Jamie lives in Connecticut with her husband and three children.

HEATHER STEVENSON is Deputy General Counsel to Boston Globe Media Partners, the parent company of *The Boston Globe*, Boston.com, and STAT. Heather started her legal career as a litigation associate at Sullivan & Cromwell in New York and is the founder of Thirst Juice Co., a plant-based juice and smoothie bar that operated in the Boston area from 2014 to 2019. She is a graduate of Columbia Law School and Columbia College and received her LLM from the University of Amsterdam.

Heather lives in the Boston area with her husband, 4-year-old son, and 12-year-old Morkie. In her free time, Heather runs marathons, travels the world, and alternates between drinking green juice and eating chocolate chip cookies.

JAMIE SZAL assists businesses in all aspects of state and local tax, from compliance to audits and administrative proceedings through litigation. Jamie is the president of the Trinity College Alumni Association, alumni liaison to the board of trustees, and a founding member of the Women's Leadership Council. She serves on the board of a dental nonprofit and serves on the MothersEsquire Program Committee, heading the Pump up the Bar campaign. She is also involved with the Maine State Bar Association Women's Law Section.

Jamie co-authored the Amazon bestseller, *#Networked*, an anthology about the power of women supporting women in a digital community. Jamie enjoys raising her fiercely independent and impish daughter, singing, and hiking with her husband, daughter, and dogs.

LAUREN A. TETENBAUM is an advocate and therapist specializing in life transitions affecting millennials and young women. With advanced training in perinatal mental health, Lauren currently provides clinical and coaching services to individuals and groups of working, new, and aspiring parents. She counsels millennials, Gen Z members, and teens on topics including relationships, career paths, and anxiety disorders. She also advises clients on workplace policy issues related to flexibility and wellness. Lauren decided to focus on counseling and consulting to fill gaps in connection and community.

Previously, Lauren spent a decade in the legal industry working with various clients at vulnerable points of their lives. She is a firstgeneration American and practiced immigration law at top firms in the United Kingdom and United States, assisting clients of myriad backgrounds in navigating complex government systems to embark on their next life chapter.

Lauren maintained an active pro bono legal practice, counseling clients fleeing persecution in their home countries, abusive romantic partners or parents, or other trauma. Lauren also worked in personnel-based roles in which she focused on professional development and mentoring. She guided lawyers adjusting to a new baby and successfully led the advocacy for a more comprehensive parental leave policy. While helping coordinate the global pro bono program of a top international law firm, Lauren worked closely with clients in need, including LGBTQ individuals and legal/social service organizations serving women and youth.

Lauren is actively involved in numerous efforts benefitting at-risk populations in her area and abroad. She is on the board of her town's League of Women Voters and chairs the community service committees at her children's schools. She also volunteers on the Postpartum Support International helpline and as a RALLY booster for The Mom Project. Lauren has been featured on several parental wellness platforms as an expert on work/life integration and regularly speaks at events on women's mental health. Lauren feels privileged to use her experience, empathy, and emotional intelligence to empower others.

Lauren holds a bachelor's, *magna cum laude,* from the University of Pennsylvania, a Master of Social Work from New York University, and a JD from the Cardozo School of Law. She resides outside her native New York City with her family.

As a licensed social worker, former BigLaw attorney, and professional coach, Lauren is also the proud mom of two young kids. She is particularly passionate about supporting and empowering working, new, and aspiring mothers.

Visit www.LATCounseling.com to learn more about her mission and counseling services.

We All Belong Here

by Heidi K. Brown[*]

> *"Let's spotlight one another's strengths, celebrate one another's authentic power, and supercharge the soul of the legal profession—forever."*

WE DRESSED IN THE requisite suits. The sensible shoes. Maybe a dash of lip gloss.

We did what was asked of us. Billed copious hours. Read the cases. Deciphered the statutes. Drafted the contracts. Solved the problems. Fought the fights.

Perhaps, at first to fit in, we tried to mirror the behavior, the mood, the timbre of our male or more senior counterparts. Possi-

---

[*] Heidi K. Brown is a law professor and former litigator in the construction industry. She received her law degree from The University of Virginia School of Law and a master's degree in applied positive psychology from the University of Pennsylvania. She is the author of *The Introverted Lawyer*, *Untangling Fear in Lawyering*, and *The Flourishing Lawyer: A Multi-Dimensional Approach to Performance and Well-Being*. She champions the importance of amplifying our advocacy voices authentically, and fostering a life of flourishing in the law.

bly, we deflected, or tolerated, some less-than-stellar behavior along the way.

We put our heads down and did the hard work.

At some point, each of us had an awakening. We started to "know thyself," as Socrates urged. We got intellectually humble and experimented with our authentic advocacy voices, our individual styles. We jettisoned the "just do it," the "fake it till we make it," and "never let them see you sweat" mantras and got real. We liked what we saw … and felt … and created.

We began rejecting the myth of "one pathway to success" in lawyering, rewriting our scripts. We reinvented ourselves. If we didn't love the initial career path we chose, we forged a new one, sometimes bushwhacking into uncharted territory—maybe even more than once. Some of us took circuitous, serpentine routes to find *our* way.

We pondered what it meant for each of us to embody "character and fitness" to practice law—not just to gain entry to the profession but *every day* thereafter. We decided what we wanted our individual lawyering *character* to look like. We redefined what *fitness*—intellectual, emotional, physical, spiritual—means to us, as individuals and as a community.

THE AUTHORS IN THIS book aspire to inspire the next generation of lawyers to realize: *The law is a new language.* It might take some of us longer than others to grasp it. Some individuals will rock law school—getting great grades, collecting accolades like membership on law review editorial boards and moot court teams, landing "prestigious" jobs.

Others of us will struggle at first to find our niche, our calling. That's perfectly okay. We each bring diverse assets to the profession—all valuable. Some of us thrive while quietly writing powerful briefs in solitude. Others of us flourish when delivering impactful arguments from a podium.

Among us are fierce negotiators, collaborative problem-solvers, deep thinkers, idea generators, innovators, helpers, nurturers, active listeners, change-makers, relationship builders, pioneers, poets, artists, rebels.

We all belong here.

Free yourself to be yourself.
If only you could see yourself.
U2

WE HOPE THE STORIES of the women in these pages empower others to design a life in the law infused with meaning, purpose, and zest. To cultivate work environments in which each of us can tap into our *individual zones of optimal functioning* (our IZOF). To foster states of *flow*—where the skills we've honed enable us to meet the challenges posed; where we're so immersed and engaged in our work that time and space seem to temporarily disappear. And we emerge from our flow zones—exhilarated and fulfilled.

Let's spotlight one another's strengths, celebrate one another's authentic power, and supercharge the soul of the legal profession—forever.

Forging Our Own Path

by Angela Han

> *"Let us celebrate each of these women as we read their stories and let them be the new examples that we look up to ..."*

IN MID-2021, I decided to gather stories from about 20 women who have created their own path in the law and make it into a book.

Why?

For the longest time, we have been told that there are limited paths to success, primarily by climbing the corporate ladder. As a society, we have celebrated women who have traveled the rare path to the C-suite, with the hope of modeling their success in claiming a coveted seat at the table.

But implicit in this narrative is that there is no other path to success available, and that is simply not true.

We do not celebrate enough the women who have decided to forge their own path, the women who were creative and bold enough to live life on their own terms. Not for the recognition or the acknowledgment but simply because this is the way that worked for them.

Women in Law Discovering the True Meaning of Success is a collection of stories of women lawyers who decided that they are successful—not because of anyone else but because of themselves. No one else was going to dictate their path for them.

Let us celebrate each of these women as we read their stories and let them be the new examples that we look up to—the examples of those whose paths we should follow but only to the extent that we celebrate our own uniqueness and not simply the path that they have forged.

These examples show that we can do anything, even if it means veering away from the beaten path—especially when it means veering away from the beaten path.

Each of these women's stories is evidence that you can create anything, even when there are no examples to look up to.

Just like the 23 of us who came together to create this book out of nothing but desire, joy, and determination.

Our Stories

CHAPTER ONE

The Fountainhead of Strength

by Christine Payne

> *"My children's mere existence makes me a better lawyer because I am hyper-focused on efficiency (so that I can maximize time with them), and because caring for them refreshes me and constantly challenges my perspective."*

LAST YEAR, I read a troubling article published in the *American Bar Association Journal*. It inspired this book. You know an article has hit a nerve when a legion of women rises up and group-writes a book to prove how wrong it is.[1] But the author's perspective, detailed in the article, was taught to all of us at one point in time, and she was simply repeating what used to be standard issue.

And, indeed, that perspective still has plenty of supporters lurking in the smoky back rooms of white-shoe law firms ...

---

[1] See the *ABA Journal* at https://www.abajournal.com/news/article/womens-success-in-legal-careers-lack-of-advancement-is-not-a-woman-problem-its-a-profession-problem. ABA President Patricia Lee Refo—along with nine former ABA presidents—wrote a strong repudiation of the article.

<<SCENE>>

Early Monday at the law offices of Scrooge & Marley.

Light filters in through cracks in the heavy silk curtains. A silver pot of fresh coffee gleams in the morning light. Scrooge reaches for his copy of the *ABA Journal* and turns to a particular article regarding women in the profession.

SCROOGE: Marley, this here article says that women are not aware of the pitfalls existing in the path from associate to partner. They are not sufficiently focused on upward mobility!

MARLEY: Yes, they have the mommy brain. It would be so much better if they could see that motherhood is a distraction that will lead them astray. It is very different than fatherhood.

SCROOGE: Maybe that darned diversity consultant was wrong! Maybe the fact that our firm leadership is now and always has been dominated by men is simply reflective of an inherent flaw in the women. It's not that they can't make it if they try—it's that they're not trying hard enough!

MARLEY: Yes, such a pity. They are their own worst enemies! But there is nothing we can do. We cannot change anything about our flawless model of promotion. I do hope that this *ABA Journal* article convinces woman lawyers to be more careful. It's written by a woman, after all!

<<SOUND: A KNOCK ON THE DOOR>>

MS. CRATCHIT: Good morning, Mr. Marley, Mr. Scrooge. I just finished the 40-page memo you requested on Friday night. It required an opinion published in a book not in our library, but I was able to locate a copy at the courthouse three towns over and coordinate with the clerk to messenger it here.

SCROOGE: Ms. Cratchit, you look disheveled and your jacket is stained. Is that yogurt?

MS. CRATCHIT: I'm so sorry; I spilled the Dannon Light & Fit® from the breakroom on myself sometime Sunday but didn't have time to return home to freshen up. I do apologize. It won't happen again.

SCROOGE: See that it doesn't.

<<MS. CRATCHIT LEAVES, THE HEAVY DOOR CLICKING BEHIND HER>>

SCROOGE: Let's remember to get rid of the yogurt. Can't be spending on frivolity that people are just going to spill.

MARLEY: Perhaps she does not have a growth mindset. She would do well to read the *ABA Journal's* article. Anyway, what is this important 40-page memo?

SCROOGE: Oh, it's something I thought of last Wednesday or Thursday, but it slipped my mind until I was leaving on Friday—it was a genius idea for one of our clients. On Saturday, however, I remembered that the client's business is about to be sold and they won't need it after all. Oh, well.

MARLEY: Do you need to spend time reading it this morning or can we go to the club?

SCROOGE: No, I may look at it later. Yes, let's go to the club. And let's ask that nice young chap who just started to join us. You know, the first-year associate—Gideon's nephew.

MARLEY: Splendid. He is a sharp young man who reminds me of myself when I was young—a real go-getter! As Lao Tzu once said, "a bright future has one who shines as a mirror to the king."

<<SCENE>>

I REJECT THE IDEA that women with children cannot successfully climb the legal career ladder and be great moms at the same time. That is old thinking derived from and designed to support the patriarchy.

My children's mere existence makes me a better lawyer because I am hyper-focused on efficiency (so that I can maximize time with them), and because caring for them refreshes me and constantly challenges my perspective.

Is it hard to handle both kids and a job in a single day? Yes. Are there things we can and should do to make it easier for working parents? Yes. Should we normalize childcare by encouraging men to actively take paternity leave and otherwise have a robust home life? Yes.

But my incredible children are not an albatross around my neck; they are the fountainhead of my strength.

Ok, enough about that *ABA Journal* article. I'm quite sure I've written some things myself that didn't reflect well on me.

IN FACT, THERE'S a letter I wrote when I was a baby lawyer—it was completely absurd. Upon receipt, opposing counsel appropriately went apoplectic. The letter was overly formalistic, bizarrely rigid, chock full of unnecessary detail, and flat-out non-collegial. What happened was this:

On behalf of our client, we had sent out some requests for production. The other side never responded. Instead of picking up the phone like a normal person and asking what was going on with the absent responses, I went full-on lawyer. I researched the rules and found out that, technically, if you don't respond to written requests for production under the time prescribed, then you've waived all your objections and must produce all responsive documents forth-with. Forthwith! I wrote all that in my letter and sent it off—terribly embarrassing in hindsight.

Looking back, it was a strange way to not only approach prac-tice (sorry to Jack Griem, wherever you are) but also to view the world and the law. I'll have to pay my therapist extra to help me work through the origins of such a weird perspective. But in terms of career development, I was just learning about litigation and col-legiality. I was just learning about this weird thing called discovery. The federal rules had been amended that year to recognize elec-tronic discovery (or eDiscovery).

I remember saying out loud, "I should become an expert in this, like ... maybe ... maybe that's the way to be valuable long term." As I uttered those words, the associate sitting in my office laughed so hard that he snorted Diet Coke through his nose. He told me that was a very bad idea.

Other than that, I don't really remember what I wanted out of my career back then. I was more focused on how to pay the bills and become stable with a young family.

I HAD A LOT OF learning to do. By that I mean learning how to handle myself in awkward situations. One time, a junior partner complained that I was too polite (and, apparently, I was—she took it as condescending). Another time, opposing counsel told me I was very smart for a woman. His colleague told me I should be a schoolteacher. How does one handle that in a conference room six floors up? So many questions and not enough answers:

- ❖ What about credit stealers?

- ❖ How do you admit when you're wrong?

- ❖ What's a big deal and what's not?

- ❖ What happens when someone you admire turns on you?

- ❖ What happens when you choke in court?

That last one has only happened to me once, but it was the most embarrassing moment in my entire life and it still haunts me.

OVER THESE SHORT 15 years, there have been some fantastic highs and some desperate lows—I have lost so much it's almost unbearable to think about. But I've gained as well, and I try to take the seasons as they come. Snapshot memories—a team breakfast before court, laughing with colleagues during late-night deadlines, meeting a client with a great sense of humor—are moments in time that are precious and can never be replicated. More great moments will come, but the feeling will never be quite the same. People move on, cases end. The only constant is change.

I never used to write these reflective pieces or subscribe to anything celebratory about my career. But a couple of years ago, I got sucked into submitting a profile to one of those women-in-the-law magazines—you know, the articles about the "best doctors in America" that you can find in the middle of airplane magazines? Those articles with pictures of people who are very clearly not the best doctors in America? It was like that, but for lawyers.

I filled out a form and my daughter helped me pick out an outfit for the photo. I didn't think she would ever remember anything about it—she was 8 years old at the time. Recently, however, a friend overheard my daughter say that her mom was an amazing lawyer and got her picture taken for "woman of the year." Inaccuracies aside, my heart was so full—my daughter remembered and was proud of me. I realized that 15 years into this career, I should be proud, too.

I HAVE CRYSTALLIZED what I want from my career (at least for now)—to lead a successful practice group focused on eDiscovery strategy, while surrounded by smart and kind colleagues and clients. I want to create a work casa where people can feel comfortable, thrive, and grow in their careers.

Oh, there's one more thing I'd like to do—help young attorneys overcome the awkward letter-writing phase.

Someone called me a mama duck the other day and I almost cried—I think it was a compliment ... I took it that way.

CHAPTER TWO

A Pioneering Personality

by Michelle Banks

"I jumped at the opportunity to become focused on helping legal leaders achieve their professional development goals. I am lucky. My passion for a long time has been to help more women reach the top of the corporate world; and, while for many years it was something I did in addition to my primary job, now it is my job and I love it."

I WAS A "FIRST GEN"—the first person in my family to graduate from law school and before that from university. In 1988, my first-year law firm associate salary blew our minds.

I was inspired to become a lawyer after interviewing my next door neighbor, a practicing lawyer, for an elementary school assignment about potential careers.

I had the confidence to take risks in my education and later in my professional career because I had substantial support from my family and other people. But I never really looked at it as taking risks; rather, I was embracing exciting opportunities.

Tests show that I am a "natural pioneer" personality. I have also adopted a growth mindset—the belief that I am not just what I am born with and that anything can be learned through continuous education, effort, and experience.

I believe that one of the most important aspects of growth mindset is learning from our mistakes. I make my fair share of mistakes. They make me more resilient and a better leader.

ONE THING I NEVER lacked was the courage to try new things and trust in my ability to succeed at whatever I choose to do. Beginning when I was a third-year law firm associate, I started taking career risks.

Each time, I lacked some experience that people may have thought was needed for a new role, but I jumped all in:

- ❖ I took a huge career leap and moved to Tokyo for one year to become the first woman lawyer in the legal department of a Japanese client of my law firm. I had no business experience whatsoever outside the United States, and I had never been to Asia.

- ❖ Mid-career, when I wanted a longer term in-house position, I took an assignment in the legal department of the Golden State Warriors NBA team, having never before attended a professional basketball game.

- ❖ When I was ready to move into management at Gap Inc., I got the promotion by asking for it and then agreeing to create the company's corporate compliance program when I barely knew what one was.

- ❖ As a last step before becoming the Chief Legal Officer, I accepted a promotion to Vice President in charge of Gap employment law—its largest, highest-risk litigation team—

when I had not been in a courtroom since the day I was sworn in as a licensed attorney over a decade earlier.

Each of these risks broadened my experience and my perspective, and in some way contributed to my becoming a Senior Corporate Legal Executive.

I DO NOT KNOW IF I would have become a Chief Legal Officer if I had not landed at Gap Inc. Two women, Anne Gust Brown and Lauri Shanahan, preceded me in the General Counsel position at Gap. They served as incredibly inspirational role models for me. They also mentored me.

Anne is a courageous powerhouse who was very active in the community. Lauri is an incredible lawyer mom who somehow coached one of her daughter's soccer teams while serving as General Counsel.

Lauri saw things in me that I did not see in myself. She pushed and supported me. Lauri was more than a mentor to me. She was definitely a sponsor, giving me more and more senior roles and visibility while also setting me up for success. They both remain friends, and Lauri continues to mentor me to this day.

But my 10 years as General Counsel of a global, high-profile, public company were not easy. During those 10 years, I had but one opportunity to completely unplug when my family and I spent four days on safari in South Africa.

I could not have succeeded at that exciting, yet overwhelming, job without the support of many people—especially my family and the very talented members of my Gap Inc. legal team. My son was only 6 years old when I became General Counsel. My mother was a tremendous help, and I am well aware that her helping to care for my family and me enabled me to lead.

My mother, Yvonne Niven, is the most loving, generous person on this planet. My sister, Yvette Hetrick, is my best friend and cheerleader. Most importantly, my husband, Lee Banks, not only puts up with me, he strongly supports me in anything and everything I do.

Lee always jokes, "We traded NBA floor seats for half off on jeans." But as my (s)hero, Justice Ruth Bader Ginsburg, once said, "I had a life partner who thought my work was as important as his, and I think that made all the difference for me." Lee throws his full support my way—no strings attached.

Until I joined Gap in 1999, I never had a manager or mentor who was a woman. For 10 years, I was professionally trained, supported, and inspired by male lawyers, such as Kirk Maeda, Robert Townsend, and Robin Baggett.

Maeda-san took a big chance on me. He hired me to be the first woman lawyer to work in the legal department at one of Japan's largest corporations.

As my boss, he fiercely advocated for me for the year that I worked there. He told everyone they not only had to work with me, they had to listen to me. He would proudly proclaim that I was the deal lead while in a room full of older Japanese male bankers. When asked how to act with the first lawyer who is also a woman, Maeda-san told the Itochu legal team to treat me exactly as they would a man.

In that era in Tokyo, the men had lockers, the women served tea. On my first day on the job, Maeda-san very publicly gave me a locker that I mostly did not know what to do with; but it was important symbolism, along with not expecting me to serve tea to the other members of the legal team twice daily.

I OFTEN HEAR AND READ—particularly in response to the #metoo movement of recent years—many men are avoiding women in the workplace. I challenge men to do the opposite. If a male lawyer could successfully manage and sponsor the first woman professional in a large Japanese corporation in 1992 with success, I am confident that every man can figure out a way to support women today in a way that works for both genders.

In Tokyo in the 1990s, gender bias was obvious. If Madea-san had not stepped up and paved a path for women lawyers, no one else would have. It may be less obvious today in some cities, but it is just as important.

It remains mostly men who are in the positions of power in our institutions, whether law firms, corporations, governments, or others. Whether you call it "He for She," "Good Guys," "Men in the Mix," or something else, it is absolutely essential to the achievement of gender parity that men champion women individually and collectively, and champion equal rights of women generally.

Twenty years after I was the first woman lawyer to work for Itochu, my friend, Claire Chino, became Itochu's General Counsel. Claire is awesome. She was not only the first female head of legal at Itochu, she was the first woman and youngest officer ever at any Japanese trading company.

I screamed out loud in my Gap office the day I received an email from Rob Townsend with the news of Claire's promotion to head Itochu's legal department. It will not surprise you that Maeda-san had been her manager and sponsor, as he was mine. When I got in my car to drive home from work that evening, I called my mom. As I shared Claire's news with her, I cried tears of joy and relief.

One of the first things I did when I retired from Gap in 2016 was take my son, husband, and parents to Tokyo to meet Maeda-san and Claire. Visiting them at Itochu was the highlight of every member of my family's trip to Japan and China to celebrate my corporate retirement.

Today, Claire is the CEO of Itochu International. The small part that I played in opening the door for women lawyers in Tokyo has been, without question, the highlight of my career.

I WORKED ACROSS THE law firm spectrum in three offices of a global firm, in the headquarters office of a national firm, and in a small firm. I did not particularly like it. It was partially the unfavorable aspects of those institutions; but it was also me.

The technical aspects of law were never my strong suit; but I did not want to be a foremost expert on legal regulations, I wanted to help people practically solve challenges.

I was happy to let go of the law library when I moved in-house.

While in corporate law practice, closing the deal and pleasing people energized me. After retiring from serving as General Counsel for 10 years, I didn't miss the prestigious title, fancy office, or powerful budget. I missed the people.

When I retired at the age of 52, many people told me I was too young to retire. My response: "It's like dog years and I'm older than I look." It's been a joy to have the privilege of retiring relatively early from practicing law to pursue my personal passions.

I HAD PROMISED MYSELF and my family I would take a full year off after retiring from Gap to sleep and exercise more, travel for fun, and spend quality time with my only child before he left for college.

In early 2017, Bob Barker approached me with an offer to help BarkerGilmore expand its service offerings from solely in-house legal and compliance recruiting to include advising legal and compliance leaders. I jumped at the opportunity to become focused on helping legal leaders achieve their professional development goals.

My passion for a long time has been to help more women reach the top of the corporate world; and, while for many years it was something I did in addition to my primary job, now it is my job and I love it. I am lucky.

WHAT I LIKED MOST ABOUT, and excelled at, being a global General Counsel was leading and mentoring a large team of people and having a wide platform from which to champion diversity, equity, and inclusion in the legal profession. It is unacceptable to me that our legal profession, which is so critical to the achievement of justice in society, is one of the least diverse white-collar professions. Our lack of inclusion prevents us from achieving the best legal solutions and leveraging the best potential talent.

I work with many organizations to try to change that paradigm. In both my business and my nonprofit board service, I have the opportunity to support a diverse set of corporate lawyers on a daily basis.

I love helping people—especially underrepresented lawyers. When Bob Barker asked me to help him start a General Counsel coaching business, I knew immediately it would be for me. And it is. I know now that this is my life's purpose.

Today, I am a mother, spouse, and daughter, an executive coach to General Counsel, and an advocate for women lawyers.

In my coaching, I typically support newer General Counsel and those who are going through other transitions, for example, going global or public, or changing industries. I also lead law department strategic meetings and professional development workshops and give keynote speeches.

On a pro bono basis, my work goes toward advancing diversity, equity, and inclusion in the legal profession through nonprofit board service, as well as mentoring and convening women lawyers.

I serve on two advisory boards at my law school, including UCLA Law Women LEAD, an initiative I co-founded and co-chair at my alma mater. I serve on the board of directors of DirectWomen, a nonprofit that supports women lawyers joining major corporate boards. I serve on the women's leadership advisory board at Orrick law firm and cohost the LadderHer Up retreat annually for Ms. JD. In both my professional and pro bono work, I enjoy helping others achieve their career goals.

As Gap founder Don Fisher famously stated: "Do What You Love." It took me 53 years to get there, but now I truly do.

CHAPTER THREE

No Silver Spoon Required

by Bellina Barrow

> *"I have realised that coaching and mentoring is not just a unique skill but an art that is wrapped up in being diplomatic and tactful, among other things. I am forever grateful for those who fulfilled that role in my career and planted seeds and/or fanned flames that contributed to my professional growth and development. From these persons, I have taken "mental notes" of the kind of leader I need to be."*

"PLAY" WAS MY MIDDLE name as a child! Just thinking about the level of activity I was involved in during my childhood, I don't know if I could have survived had the Coronavirus pandemic taken place while I was growing up! I played marbles, cricket, basketball, football, jumped rivers, rode bicycles, climbed fruit trees, scaled fences, threw boomerangs (which once ended up on the neighbour's roof), walked to the arcade after school to play video games, mostly with the boys from my neighbourhood or my co-ed, public primary school, Arima New Government School (in Trinidad & Tobago, West Indies). It's obvious that I was a bit of a tomboy (not so much now), and I talk about sports equally and sometimes more than I talk about law because sports taught me how to handle myself in many situations and how to treat people I would encounter in my life and career.

With my father's leading and encouragement, I channeled my love for play into organised sport as a pre-teen and teenager by focusing on tennis and table tennis. I then scaled down to just table tennis in the early 1990s; and most of my Easter and summer vacations were spent training, travelling, and competing at various tournaments to represent my country. It was through representing my country, university, and high school at tournaments that lessons about loyalty, teamwork, strategy, compassion, integrity, fair play, patriotism, and being gracious in defeat were ingrained in me. So, all my summer vacations (or, as we would say in my country, August holidays) spent in table tennis training and competition manifested in a really meaningful way in my life, as the lessons would come in very handy in my professional life.

As early as I can remember, I was argumentative and had a retort for everything when I was a child. So it didn't come as a surprise when as a teenager in high school at St. Joseph's Convent, Port-of-Spain, I unequivocally and unreservedly articulated to a local newspaper journalist that I wanted to be a lawyer and work for the United Nations when I grew up. Although that was captured in the 1990s during a sports interview (I was then a junior national table tennis player), it was my first major shot at career goal-setting and I didn't even realise it!

BEFORE BEING ADMITTED to legal practice in Trinidad & Tobago, I had a local and international career in human resources (HR). HR was not actually my preferred area of study and choice of profession. But I wasn't accepted into the law program on my initial applications to University of the West Indies, St. Augustine,

Trinidad. As such, I selected a government degree (generally likened to political science) as my second choice program of study. Along the way in the government degree, I chose courses for minors in human resource management and management information systems. My minor in human resource management helped with employability as I was selected for summer internships in that field and landed HR jobs in the United Kingdom and in Trinidad.

My time in HR aided my personal and professional life through all the skills it has taught me about the HR function; knowledge that I have transferred to related areas of legal practice, *e.g.*, labour & employment law. It has made me more discerning of processes, practices, and environments for my own life decisions. Additionally, it taught me to treat each person fairly, giving them a chance and not being an obstacle in their path to potential opportunity, growth, or progress.

While in the United Kingdom, I applied for the law program back home, with no real expectation that I would be accepted. As fate would have it, when I returned to Trinidad & Tobago and was settled in a decent HR role there, I received the acceptance letter from the University of the West Indies. I was of two minds as to whether I should disrupt my current career trajectory to undertake this new line of study. I mean, human resources had granted me many unforgettable experiences, *i.e.*, recruiting a formerly imprisoned person and working with job applicants from all walks and stages of life and all corners of the globe (some even non–English-speaking).

Further to this, it taught me to be tolerant, humane, non-biased, non-partisan, and non-judgmental. However, my father encouraged me and made me aware of the fact that many lawyers, particularly in the United States, pursued other first degrees and careers before pursuing a career in law. So I resigned from my HR role and proceeded with my law studies with that in mind.

My law journey has had a large dose of failures, loss, grief, and a host of other adversities that could have made me throw in the towel. But if there is one thing that my primary school's watch-words taught me was that "Perseverance Wins!"

I PURSUED MY LAW DEGREE at the University of the West Indies. It was there that I had my first taste at failing a course during my tertiary-level studies. Receiving the news of that course failure was crushing. All the way home, I had thoughts of self-doubt and defeat and I deliberated whether I was meant to be studying law at all. However, I had to shelve those self-defeating thoughts as these would impact my performance in my courses for the semester that was still in session. I completed my exams for that semester and thereafter focused on my preparations for the summer supplementary exam for the course I had failed. I passed all my courses for that semester and my supplementary exam. Luckily, I had no shockers for the other two years of my law studies and I successfully completed my law degree in 2010. Thereafter, I returned to Trinidad to begin the second part of my qualification process to become an attorney—two years of law school.

The intensity increased several notches at law school and I don't quite think the law degree was adequate preparation or a fair indication of the demands and rigours that would come during law school. During my first week at the Hugh Wooding Law School in St. Augustine, Trinidad, I had second thoughts as to whether I could overcome the new and challenging demands that were being presented. It was probably here that I heard reiterated more times than ever: "The law is a jealous mistress!" I cannot say where the thoughts of giving up went after the first week. I guess eventually I found my footing, got in a groove, and tried to maintain balance in the face of the demands of the curriculum.

I had a second dose of failing a course at law school. This experience was different. For most of my law degree, while I was studying in Barbados, my father was battling cancer. My family members, back home, were largely handling hospital trips, treatment, getting medication, etc., while I was in Barbados. I joined in my father's health care journey in 2010 when I returned to Trinidad.

However, in 2011, my father's health took a turn for the worse. During my end of year-one exams, I stayed with my godmother closer to my law school for ease of exam preparation and to obviate the need for a long commute. The afternoon before my final exam was unsettling and distracting. I was not sure about my sister's ground transport arrangements from the airport as she was scheduled to be visiting from abroad. So while studying on campus, I left to go home to see if she had arrived. I had not seen my father for my entire exam period as I would just check in with him by phone and he was not one to offload his burdens on anyone who called him. He was always doing "pretty good" whenever anyone spoke to him.

During that brief visit home, I could see he had lost a lot of weight and his gait and stance were much weaker. That image of my father was imprinted on my mind for the entire drive back to my godmother's home and during the night when I was trying to complete my final preparation for the exam the next morning. That image could not be erased from my head. Throughout my exam, I was in a daze—simple principles and cases escaped me; and I am not quite sure what I really wrote on that exam paper. While I was disappointed when I failed that course, the failure did not demoralise me in light of my state of mind leading up to and during that exam, probably because it was a course I quite enjoyed (as it was taught by a female lawyer and my former supervisor whom I hold in high regard).

I vowed to prepare for and re-sit the exam during the summer supplemental exams in the midst of my In-service Training—a mandatory period of attachment that I did at a law chamber in Port-of-Spain, Trinidad, in July 2011. With the help of very supportive classmates who were trainees with me at the same law chamber, my preparation for the exam re-sit was promising, tolerable, and bearable. Even though I had to do the exam myself, I never felt like I was walking that road alone.

July 2011 would not be uneventful though. Soon after getting into the office one morning, I received a call from my mother saying that my father had to be rushed to the hospital. One of my supervising attorneys, recognising that the news was too much for me to bear, insisted that I go home. He also allowed my two friends who were in training with me to accompany me home. Thereafter, my father continued to be in and out of the hospital and I accompanied and supported my mother during that period. The night of July 7, 2011, would be the last time I would see my father alive as he passed away at the hospital during the day on July 8, before I could return to the hospital to visit him.

In returning to the office after my father's funeral, my friends asked if I was sure I still wanted to repeat the course that summer instead of doing it during the next term. I was adamant I was not repeating the course in the school term, as I did not want to add an additional course to the already heavy and demanding course load of the school term. I stuck to my decision, my friends continued to support and encourage me through it all, and I excelled at my supplementary exam that summer.

It was not all doom and gloom as I have very fond memories of law school—I reminisce about the different Caribbean nation events, our sports day, and our Christmas production. It was during law school that I also recommenced my volunteer and community service in the group, Beautiful Struggle Foundation, particularly by assisting with charity drives and youth motivational speaking. My legal education culminated in May 2012 when I completed my year-two exams at Hugh Wooding Law School.

In November 2012, I was admitted to legal practice in Trinidad & Tobago. This came to fruition through faith, perseverance, the support of loyal family and loved ones (past and present), friends, bursaries, student loans, government education subvention programs, and savings and internship stipends.

There was no silver spoon.

FROM 2013 TO 2014, I represented corporate and individual clients as an associate attorney at a small law firm in Port-of-Spain, Trinidad. I got my feet wet and started to improve on and develop my skills to the point where I would regularly advocate in matters at the High and Magistrate's Courts. This was a baptism of fire. It came with the constant curveballs and unhelpful undercurrents from opposing counsel and the occasional rebuke by some judges.

Of my memorable moments, I recall two notable victories, one involving a non-contact road traffic accident and the other an insurance matter on the issue of "without prejudice" communication— the latter of which resulted in my first written judgment. In the midst of those learning curves and highs, there would come another curveball. I would experience the loss of my significant other when he suffered the return of a cancerous brain tumor. He passed away on December 5, 2013.

By August 2014, I decided I was ready to move on from this role at my first law firm in Trinidad & Tobago. Just before the last quarter of 2014, by pure chance, I got the opportunity to move to Antigua & Barbuda. I had submitted an online application for an associate role without paying particular attention to the location of the job. When I was invited to interview via Skype (which was popular then), the location was made clear to me. That didn't deter me because living in a foreign country was not novel to me. While I had never been to Antigua & Barbuda, it is a Caribbean island with a largely similar climate; and it also is a Commonwealth Caribbean legal jurisdiction. I knew I could do this!

In 2014, in the process of preparing my court documents for my Antigua & Barbuda admission to legal practice, I visited a law office in Port-of-Spain, Trinidad, where the notary public/attorney was my father's longtime friend. We had never met, but while notarising the documents, he engaged me in conversation as to my surname and made the connection between the families. After he completed notarisation, in response to my enquiry about his fees, he said, "There is no fee. Just continue to make your father proud." I knew I was doing something good in my legal journey and that I should continue in this vein based on these words of encouragement.

While at the firm in Antigua & Barbuda, I practised for over four years representing corporate and individual clients. As in Trinidad, I made individual court appearances and also instructed Senior/Queen's counsel and senior attorneys in diverse matters at the High Court.

In Antigua, I began appearing and instructing Senior/Queen's counsel and senior attorneys at the Industrial Court and Court of Appeal. One of my early notable moments in practice in Antigua & Barbuda was my first written judgment where I instructed my then–managing partner in a successful court application involving an ancillary defendant seeking relief from sanctions and an extension of time to file an ancillary defence. This subsequently resulted in the ancillary claim against the ancillary defendant being discontinued and settled after mediation.

I quite enjoyed having two legal interns accompany and assist me with court matters and I also enjoyed imparting the knowledge and guidance I had learnt along my brief journey to them. I cherished the unique experiences and friendships I had developed while living in Antigua.

After taking such a deep dive into litigation, I realised I needed to gear down, even if momentarily, from the litigation pace and demands. After an enlightening, challenging, and enjoyable four-plus years of legal practice in Antigua & Barbuda,[2] I listened to my intuition and body and resigned from my role in Antigua to return to Trinidad & Tobago at the end of 2018.

At the beginning of 2019, I commenced volunteering at a community home work centre at a local primary school. Being around such a lively, loving, intelligent bunch of children was refreshing and enlightening but equally saddening when my visits to the homework centre were halted during the country's first Coronavirus pandemic lockdown in March 2020.

Later in 2019, I took on an in-house counsel role in the financial services sector until just before mid-2021. In 2020, I started to volunteer at my local bar association, the Law Association of Trinidad & Tobago, as a member of the Corporate Commercial and Conveyancing Committee. During that year, I also became a published legal author with my first legal article, "T&T After COVID-

---

[2] This experience came complete with my first, serious, solo tropical storm and hurricane experiences: Tropical Storm Gonzalo in 2014 and Hurricanes Irma and Maria in 2017.

19,"[3] and I also co-authored the legal article, "A Word To Be Cyber Wise."[4]

Having resigned from my in-house counsel role, I am focusing now on my independent legal practice and personal and professional development in a more controlled, self-determined, fulfilling, and autonomous manner.

ARISING FROM THE adversities were the lessons I consider to be the key indicators of success. Throughout what I still consider to be a very short legal career, my successes have come from:

❖ Continually working on improving aspects of legal practice that are not my strong suit and getting some court wins along the way;

❖ Relocating to a new country and learning the legal practice and culture in that jurisdiction;

❖ Incorporating lessons learnt from HR and sports in my practice of law;

❖ Constantly applying a lesson in humility of "not letting the euphoria go to my head" taught to me by my mother when I had passed for my first-choice high school in the early 1990s;

❖ Continuing to make my father proud;

---

[3] Published in AmCham *T&T Linkage* Magazine on June 2, 2020.

[4] Published on June 27, 2020, in the *Organisation of Commonwealth Caribbean Bar Associations Journal*, Vol. 2 No. 1 (January–June 2020).

❖ Making career decisions that were best for my progress, development, and wellbeing;

❖ Continuously stamping out and silencing the noise of naysayers by charting and running my own course in life and in law; and

❖ Making time to give of my time, talent, and treasure to the profession, community, and society.

I give thanks to my faithful family and loved ones (past and present), friends, lawyer mums, other authentic female lawyers, and even those male lawyers who have gone above and beyond to assist me in the profession and shown genuine, considerable interest in my career progression.

In working with these lawyer leaders, some of them inspired me through their humility, loyalty, integrity, legal acuity, tech-savviness, tenacity, compassion, emotional intelligence, coaching, and mentorship. I have realised that coaching and mentoring is not just a unique skill but an art that is wrapped up in being diplomatic and tactful, among other things. I am forever grateful for those who fulfilled that role in my career and planted seeds and/or fanned flames that contributed to my professional growth and development. From these persons, I have taken "mental notes" of the kind of leader I need to be.

My full legal story is yet to be told! With a general lifelong interest in technology, in the short and medium term, I aspire to create and be in an environment where law and technology intersect. This would be a progressive workspace where modern (legal) technology and processes are embraced, incorporated, and translate into "smarter" legal practices and processes. As such, I anticipate that I will continue on that legal course amidst all the other exciting things that are still in store for my legal practice and career. While in the long term, I aspire to be a judicial officer at either an international or local court or tribunal.

Catch me in a few years as my story continues to unfold!

CHAPTER FOUR

A Change in Attitude

by Jennifer Belmont Jennings

"There are days when I don't feel successful, and I have to tell myself to stop listening to the noise. I get to do a job I love. THAT is success. I am helping people. THAT is success. I am always learning. THAT is success. I always take advantage of opportunities to grow. THAT is success."

I REMEMBER LOOKING AT the *U.S. News and World Report* salary range for graduates from the Washington University in St. Louis School of Law. "Ok, so even if I'm on the low end I could live with my parents and pay $150,000 plus interest pretty quickly," I naïvely thought to myself. This was for the fall of 2006. Never mind that I hadn't bothered to ask my parents how they felt about this plan. If you know what happened in 2007, you'll know that my thought process went from naïve to laughable!

What became clear during the 2007–08 global financial crisis was that I'd be lucky to even find someone willing to pay me anything, let alone give me a BigLaw fancy office and salary—you know, the salary my husband assumed would pay off all that debt when he asked me to marry him when I was a 2L. We got married in January of my third year, and before I knew it, I had a bunch of fancy letters after my name, no job, and a pile of student loans that was more than the mortgage on my first house. I even went to a Halloween party after I graduated wearing a sign that said, "JD: Just Debt, MA: Money AWOL," to highlight what those fancy degrees had gotten me.

Fortunately, thanks to a family connection, I landed a job as a political research associate right after I took the bar exam. If you wanted to run for political office, I would find out everything you and your grandmother did so you could prepare for what's coming, or I would help develop material to throw at your political opponent. Quite fascinating work (though it made me never want to run for office); but a little less than a year in, I was laid off due to the economy.

IT WAS VIRTUALLY impossible to find a job in the industry. I would occasionally help my dad in the family party rental business so I could make those huge student loan payments. Do you know what it's like to wait in an unemployment line as a newly licensed attorney and graduate of a top 20 school? I do! After nearly three months, I began working for a boutique law firm doing estate planning, probate, and family law.

I enjoyed the estate planning and probate work—the family law not so much. I didn't enjoy it, but I was passionate about it. I felt I *could* do it, but the stress of litigation over children was tearing me apart due to the brokenness of our system. At first, I envisioned fixing it. I quickly realized I could not.

Then we had a baby (our son is incredible). Thankfully, I'm married to a true partner so I certainly wasn't bearing a disproportionate share of the responsibilities at home; yet I was tired. I was stressed. I couldn't sleep when I had litigious cases. My husband, worried I would suffer a heart attack in my thirties and leave him a single parent, suggested I explore other opportunities.

I found it surprisingly difficult to find a job in 2013. I was competing against people with 10-plus years of experience. I remember getting turned down for a clerk position in the County Court. I actually called the human resources person and told him he'd made a mistake, that I was "perfect" for the job. In hindsight, I'm thankful he chuckled a bit and told me how he appreciated my enthusiasm, but they had a ridiculous number of applicants with far more experience than I had—for a job that wasn't supposed to require 10-plus years of experience.

OK, SO MAYBE I needed to start looking outside the box, but what would people think? How could I even contemplate doing something other than practicing law after I spent all that time and money becoming a lawyer? Would people see me as a failure? I felt like God had literally opened every door for me to go to law school, but now all I faced were dead ends and disappointment.

So, what else can an attorney do? I like rules, so I decided to give compliance a try. A friend's father who is a financial advisor worked at a big company, so I asked if he knew anyone in the corporate office. In a surprising turn of events, he thought my estate planning background would make me a great fit for his profession. My first reaction was, "I don't want to sell stuff." I didn't want to be the person everyone avoided at cocktail parties. He assured me I wouldn't have to, so I gave it a chance.

It was suggested that I work as a Client Associate while obtaining my various licenses, and then I could transition to advisor. I traded in my nice law firm office with windows for a cubicle. I went from having an assistant to essentially being the assistant. Not exactly the path to "Supreme Court Justice" I had envisioned.

And wouldn't you know that new administrative position paid me about $20,000 more per year than the law firm. Frankly, I was thankful someone was willing to pay me. I answered the phone with a smile. I did my best to hide my insecurity and figured out a way to drop the fact that I was a lawyer into every professional conversation. (Ok, I still do that now, but it's quite relevant to my line of work.)

It took nearly two years to transition from Client Associate to advisor due to red tape, but it finally happened. I was so thankful to be able to move to an office and start work in my new role. Unfortunately, we had a lot of difficulty finding someone to fill my previous position. I ended up performing two jobs for quite some time, which really kept me from advancing. While I learned a lot, it quickly became clear that I needed to look elsewhere in order to grow. It's worth noting that what I learned was invaluable for my next role. I saw firsthand how vital that support is to success in this industry.

I looked at internal corporate opportunities, talked to law firms, talked to trust companies, and talked to other financial firms. I was having a really difficult time. Almost everything was a "not yet" or "we would love to have you, but we can only pay you XY." (I left out the "Z" because it wasn't enough to even warrant a third example letter.) I didn't want to leave just for the sake of leaving, so I had my few "Cousin Eddie" moments where I decided to hold out for "management."

I felt defeated. My attitude wasn't exactly inspired by Pollyanna. I knew I had so much to offer, but for some reason, I just kept hitting the wall of rejection. It was difficult to avoid slipping into that victim mentality at times.

Interestingly, people who didn't offer me jobs started to share my name with other people they thought might be interested in me. Some of those introductions also led to disappointment, or numerous "drag you through the mud" interviews before the disappointment. I'm pretty sure at some point every person in St. Louis knew I was looking for a new job!

I DON'T REMEMBER EXACTLY what it was, but I know I was at a low point and didn't know what else I could do. I felt so embarrassed. I felt so small. I prayed. I networked. I got frustrated. I prayed some more—a lot more! Then I had that lightbulb moment. I was doing everything I knew without the results I wanted, so what else was there left for me to do? There was only one thing in this entire situation I could control and change—my attitude. Yes, I needed an attitude change.

I made the decision to show up every day, take care of clients, and give them my best. I soaked up every learning opportunity my employer had to offer. I continued to network. I had to trust the right thing would come along at the right time.

It wasn't long after my attitude shift that I received a text from a good lawyer friend. She told me someone had asked her about me (because they kept hearing my name around town) and wanted permission to share my contact information. It was either that afternoon or the next that I found myself sitting in a beautiful conference room with two of the leading ladies in the financial industry, Barbara Archer and Carol L. Rogers. By the end of our meeting, I was being shown what would be my office.

I also happened to be in a potential job conversation with a wonderful woman, now friend, at another firm in St. Louis. When I mentioned I had been given an offer to work with Barbara and

Carol, she said I *"had* to take it."* She could not let me pass up that opportunity. I'll be forever grateful that she wanted what was best for me, even if it meant a bit more of a delay for her to hire someone on her team.

What was the lesson? Even though I endured some difficult times, I could clearly see that each step truly was a building block to get me to the right place. Even when a task seemed trivial, it helped me become better at my job. Every single step (or even what felt like a step back) in my career path was important, even when it didn't feel like it. You can't always see it in the moment, but it's a lesson I hope to never forget when the next challenge comes along—and there will be a challenge!

IT DIDN'T TAKE ME long to realize that Hightower Wealth Advisors | St. Louis was the place for me. It was almost a hybrid between a financial firm and a law firm. I was able to put my legal background to use by being more involved in the client estate planning process; and we were much more focused on comprehensive financial planning, which requires a deeper dive into estate and tax planning with clients and their estate planning attorneys and tax professionals. Law school wasn't a complete waste of money after all.

Additionally, a nonprofit I was introduced to through my previous place of employment, Fathers and Families Support Center, asked me to serve on its board of directors—an opportunity that never would have come had I not been willing to set my pride aside and do something different. What a rewarding and enlightening experience that has been! I have since joined the boards of YouthBridge Community Foundation and Rooted Sisters—two other wonderful local nonprofits.

I also agreed to get the CFP® certification within my first year at Hightower. What was I thinking? My husband said I was more excited when I passed that exam than I was when I passed the bar exam! To be fair, this time, I had a family and a full-time job while trying to study for a serious exam. I was also 10 years older! He told me to "NEVER run out of the house screaming like that again unless I was being chased by a murderer," because I scared him so much with my ecstatic (and relieved) reaction.

One of the most exciting moments of my career came when I found out I was named a *St. Louis Business Journal* "40 under 40 in 2020." The celebration was short lived as we entered COVID lockdown two seconds later, but it was a moment I wouldn't have believed possible only a few years earlier. If this wasn't validation that there is life outside of BigLaw, I don't know what is!

Despite that award, I still question my "success" at times. There are days when I don't feel successful, and I have to tell myself to stop listening to the noise. I get to do a job I love. THAT is success. I am helping people. THAT is success. I am always learning. THAT is success. I always take advantage of opportunities to grow. THAT is success.

Are there difficult times? Yes. Will I always feel like I have success in every area of my life at once? Of course, not. But I've learned that success is tied to more than how many assets I have under management, how many times I'm a podcast guest, how many LinkedIn or Instagram followers I have (hope you're following me), or what my salary is. It's easy to experience swings, especially when everyone else seems to have it all together on social media. (FYI: they don't all have it together.) I'm writing this as a reminder to myself just as much as I hope it encourages you!

WE ALL KNOW THAT COVID has been a challenge (an obvious understatement). It forced most of us to "pivot." I know that's a love or hate term, but what else are you going to call it? We were all moving in one direction and then we had to shift. I felt like I was finally hitting my stride when I won my award in 2020. I could walk into a networking event and feel comfortable. I was no longer intimidated. Then, COVID. I disappeared from the public eye like everyone else and there went some of my confidence.

That's when I started writing. Rather than only writing the occasional article on investments, estate planning, and tax issues, I started to write about what it was like working from home. I joined some lawyer mom networking groups and started to write a little more. Writing became an outlet. Online networking became an outlet. (So did Peloton™, but I'll spare you the trip down that rabbit hole.)

I connected with other women lawyers and professionals through my lawyer mom Facebook groups. I really wanted to network more, and someone suggested I read the book, *#Networked*, which was written by 20 women lawyers during the pandemic about how they grew personally and professionally through their relationships on LinkedIn.

I started connecting with some of those women on LinkedIn by commenting on their posts. Before I knew it, I was in group chats and hosting Clubhouse rooms with them, and now I'm writing a chapter for this book. Though we haven't met in person (yet), these women have been an incredible benefit to my professional and personal development. I probably talk about them at home more than people I know in real life. These women understand what I'm going through. Knowing that I'm not alone in the ups and downs of trying to navigate family and career during a global pandemic is quite comforting!

MY PATH TO "SUCCESS" has been anything but what I envisioned when I began law school, but without all those bumps in the road and unexpected turns, I probably wouldn't be writing a chapter for a book! I might not be as much help to someone struggling to find their way had I not experienced that same struggle.

I've also learned an incredible amount through my experience, and I hope you'll benefit from a few extra words of self-proclaimed wisdom:

❖ You can't sit and wait for people to discover what you have to offer—you must put yourself out there and show them!

❖ You can't let the fear of what people will think stop you. No matter what you choose, some people will agree with you and some won't, so you might as well try to find something you'll enjoy.

❖ Be yourself—even if others may perceive you as marching to the beat of your own drum. The legal and financial world is full of dark suits. I wear a lot of pink and plaid with confidence!

❖ Try not to focus too much on yourself. People are coming to you for help. Making others the focus will go a long way!

❖ There is not one "right" way. Ignore the noise. Everyone is going to have an opinion. You need to learn whose opinion is worth listening to, and that does take a little experience, but you'll figure it out!

❖ You can love what you do and work a lot! There is no perfect job that is going to pay you a ton of money to feel like you're on vacation all the time–unless you're a travel writer, I suppose! Do they get paid well?

❖   Success does NOT happen overnight regardless of how it may appear on social media. You may have to do something that is less than ideal at one point or another, but how you view that experience is your choice! Let that experience make you better instead of bitter.

❖   Oh, and don't ignore planning for retirement! Start early! I know the point of this book is about a different kind of success, but you had to know I'd try to work in some financial responsibility one way or another, right?

I'm grateful to wake up each morning excited about the opportunity to engage, educate, encourage, and empower people when it comes to managing their finances. My current day looks completely different from what I envisioned in the fall of 2006, and I'm so thankful it does!

Thank you to my incredible family for all the love and support as you walked by my side (and continue to do so) during this journey!

CHAPTER FIVE

Fulfillment Through Compassion

by Jenn Deal

> *You must define what success looks like for you. You decide how you want to experience this one beautiful life. That decision is yours and yours alone. You make the rules.*

I DIDN'T ALWAYS WANT to be a lawyer. Before my junior year of college, I had repeatedly said I wasn't going to be a lawyer. I was a contrarian as a kid. I would argue about anything. You know those kids ... the ones people tell, "I bet you're going to be a lawyer when you grow up," because they don't know how to politely tell a little kid to stop being a pain in the butt.

That kid was me.

So, of course, I decided that becoming a lawyer was exactly what I wasn't going to do.

Yet, somehow, I found myself taking the LSAT toward the end of college. Why?

- ❖ In part because I thought being a lawyer sounded fancy, and I could make a lot of money.

- ❖ In part because I was really good at school.

- ❖ In part because I didn't know what else to do with my life, and I wasn't quite ready to get a full-time job and be an adult.

- ❖ In part because I took one criminal law class in college that I found fascinating.

- ❖ In part because I read too much John Grisham as a kid. (Kidding. There's no such thing as too much John Grisham.)

There were lots of reasons—none of them a great basis for making a career choice.

I came into law school having no idea what it looked like to be a lawyer. I definitely had no idea what it looked like to be a "successful" lawyer. Before I started, just the idea that I could one day refer to myself as a lawyer seemed like success. But I quickly internalized the path to success that many law schools tout: BigLaw.

Going into my first round of on-campus interviews (OCI) after my first semester, I still didn't really know what BigLaw was. I just knew I needed it.

It even sounded impressive. If you're going to do law, why not make it BIG? Go big or go home. That's what success is, right? Doing the most impressive thing you can and doing it perfectly or not bothering. That's what I had spent my whole life believing.

After just a few months in law school, I understood the "path" to success and the "plan" to get there.

And I followed the plan to a T:

- ❖ I got the grades.
- ❖ I got the BigLaw OCI interviews.
- ❖ I got the BigLaw summer associate job.
- ❖ I got the federal clerkship.
- ❖ I got the permanent BigLaw associate job.
- ❖ I made partner.

I am the consummate gold star grabber. And I am very good at it.

Here's the thing though: None of it made me feel good for more than a fleeting second. Don't get me wrong, I felt proud of each accomplishment. But the overwhelming emotion for me was relief followed by disappointment—relief that I had managed to do the thing that I was supposed to ... that I didn't fail; followed by disappointment that I felt the same. That I wasn't happy or fulfilled yet.

Then I moved on to the next goal.

Always sure the next one would be the right one.

ONCE I MADE PARTNER in 2018, the only way I can describe how I felt was untethered. There was fanfare. There were beautiful events. There were kind and heartfelt words of congratulations from my incredible colleagues, family, and friends.

After the celebration was over, all I could think was ... what's next?

I had done all the things I set out to do. Yet, I still felt the same. What was I looking for? More awards or recognition? Managing partner status? My name on the door? A SCOTUS gig?

I had gone big. And it wasn't satisfying. It didn't feel any different. I just wanted someone to tell me what THE gold star was that I needed to grab to be successful enough to finally feel fulfilled.

You've probably guessed that I am an overachiever. And I'm very good at achieving. I bet you are, too.

Merriam-Webster's Dictionary defines an overachiever as "one who achieves success over and above the standard or expected level."

Sounds pretty good, right?

Of course, it does. We live in a society obsessed with achieving. Overachieving = succeeding. It's so baked into our brains that we believe it is unarguably true. A fact. Not a story. The conditioning can be unavoidable. And subconscious.

Overachievers are smart. We quickly learn to follow the rules at home and in school. We are taught that if we follow the rules, we succeed. If we succeed, we earn praise. If we earn praise, we know we are worthy human beings.

We internalize "success" as it has been defined for us. And we internalize that meeting the external definition of "success" is how we become worthy; how we become enough.

So you get good grades in elementary school. You follow all the rules. You make the honor roll. You have great attendance. You win awards and accolades. You repeat it in middle school. Then do the same in high school. You get into a good college and repeat the cycle there.

Rinse and repeat … until that internalization is so deep that you don't realize there are other options.

And then there's law school. From the second the path to "success" as a lawyer was laid out for me (*i.e.,* the BigLaw partner path), I never once considered other options. My brain fully believed that

I was doing all the right things to succeed. I was following all the rules. There would be a reward of everlasting contentment if I was just successful enough—and successful in the "right" way.

I was wrong.

I actually started to realize I might be wrong before I made partner—as the partnership process was underway. It's not that I wasn't looking forward to making partner, I was. But I was finally starting to see that grabbing the gold stars wasn't going to change anything about the way I felt on a regular basis. The next title, the next promotion, the next positive review—they weren't going to change the feelings I was experiencing each day. I didn't know what the answer was, but I was starting to understand that it wasn't what I'd spent my whole life believing.

That's when I stumbled across life coaching.

I had a vague (uninformed idea) of what a life coach is. I'd been to presentations given by a couple of coaches, and I was not impressed. There was talk of journaling, breath work, meditations, morning routines, and positive affirmations—most of which I actually like and do now.

I'm definitely not knocking it if it works for you. But at the time, I absolutely rolled my eyes. It sounded fluffy. Not for me. As someone who suffers from an anxiety disorder and bouts of depression, I was not interested in having someone tell me that all my problems would be solved with bubble baths, thinking positive thoughts, creating the perfect morning routine, and meditating. Hiring a coach was not a consideration.

SOMEHOW THOUGH, THE UNIVERSE pointed me in the right direction. I came across a podcast called Unf*ck Your Brain by Kara Loewentheil. She had her undergraduate degree from Yale, a JD from Harvard, clerked for the U.S. Court of Appeals for the Fifth Circuit, had a prestigious academic fellowship, and was now a life coach. She is also a feminist and uses my favorite swear word unabashedly in the title of her podcast.

I was hooked. Every podcast episode felt like she was inside my brain. And every episode offered me a tool or multiple tools that I could actually use.

She showed me what my brain was doing and why.

She showed me how to start challenging the thoughts my brain offered me.

She showed me that external circumstances don't cause my feelings; the way I think about those external circumstances does. And I have a lot of control over what I decide to think, what I decide to believe.

She showed me that I could create the life I want and I could do big things without shame, self-loathing, stress, anxiety, and overwhelm.

She showed me how to feel my feelings for the first time in my life instead of avoiding them, reacting to them, or buffering or numbing them away.

There was zero fluff—just direct, brilliant, and funny discussions about human brains and their shenanigans. It was about how to manage your mind and feel your feelings, how women are socialized, and how it works to our detriment. I felt seen and heard in a way I never had.

I joined her small group program and spent six months being blown away by the things I was learning and the shifts I was able to make in my life. Over the next year, my life radically shifted in so many ways.

I shifted it … with my brain.

I felt more in control of my thoughts and emotions.

I felt more compassion for myself.

But I was still really struggling to apply that work to my career. I struggled to separate my value as a human being from my productivity, titles, achievements, and accolades; to manage my anxiety, fear, doubt, and guilt; to set boundaries and keep them; to pay attention to how I was feeling and why.

There were some shifts for sure, but I still felt I wasn't successful enough, hadn't worked hard enough, hadn't achieved enough, and wasn't perfect enough. I didn't know what "enough" was. But I still thought (or hoped) it was out there.

Then came 2020. And the introspection that came with everything that happened in 2020. And with the worst mental health crisis I've ever experienced.

It wasn't the first time I'd gone down this hole. But this time, it brought me to my knees, figuratively; but some days, literally. It forced me to reconsider how I defined success. It made me take a long hard look at my life and how I'd gotten to where I am, what I liked and didn't like, and what I wanted and didn't want.

It made me think about my values, who I am, who I'm not, who I want to be, and how I want this next part of my life to look.

Something had to change—or I was going to sell all my stuff and travel the country in a van. (A plan that is still not off the table, but it now comes from a much less desperate place.)

I had to redefine success—on my terms.

So I hired my first 1:1 coach: Olivia Vizachero of The Less Stressed Lawyer. And I used the skills I learned from my coaching sessions (along with some much-needed help from my psychiatrist and some SSRIs and SARIs to get me back to a functional baseline) to change my WHOLE life, including my career and how I experienced it.

I used coaching to do something I had never done before.

To look at my life and decide what I actually wanted it to look like. What I cared about. What I considered successful.

Here's what success looks like for me in this season of my life:

❖ Becoming a certified life coach and starting my own business coaching high-achieving women.

❖ Taking guilt-free vacations and weekends.

❖ Setting boundaries and keeping them.

❖ Asking for what I need and want.

❖ Recognizing how I'm thinking and how it is impacting my feelings, how I'm showing up, and the results I'm getting in my life.

❖ Investing in my greatest asset, me (and my brain).

❖ Sharing my thoughts, story, and coaching via social media.

❖ Crafting a legal career that I want, with intention.

❖ Crafting a life that I want, with intention.

❖ Becoming an entrepreneur and building my coaching business.

❖ Empowering other women in any way I can.

❖ Becoming more decisive.

❖ Getting rid of the Sunday Scaries.

❖ Creating deeper relationships with new and old friends.

❖ Ditching the self-judgment, blame, and shame.

❖ Being intentional with my finances so I have the freedom to continue redefining success in whatever way I want.

❖ Trusting myself and having my own back in a way that I never thought was possible.

❖ Unwinding my social conditioning.

❖ Feeling my most negative emotions, not judging them for existing, and not letting them hold me back from creating the life I want.

❖ Saying "no" to things that aren't a "hell yes" without fear or guilt.

❖ Figuring out what a "hell yes" for me even looks like.

Some of these things I'm already doing well. Some of them are still a work in progress and probably always will be.

But they are all MY choice. MY goals. MY desires.

And what I know now is that I get to redefine success any time I want. I expect that I will redefine it countless times—from year to year; day to day; minute to minute. And that both excites and scares the hell out of me.

I WAS VERY WRONG for a very long time about what success means.

If you think there is a certain way that success looks and that if you figure out what that is and achieve it, you will feel good … you are wrong, too. I say that with all the love in the world.

It's great that you are wrong. It's going to change your life once you fully accept it.

And here's the thing I want to make clear for those of you who have taken or are considering taking the BigLaw partner path: The path was not what left me feeling untethered.

It didn't matter which path I took. As long as I was using someone else's metrics for success, instead of my own, the result was always going to be the same: Dissatisfaction.

But I wouldn't go back and change my BigLaw path. I'm now practicing in an area of law that I find fascinating and challenging. I work with some of the most incredible, brilliant, multi-faceted, and kind people I've ever met. I've created deep and meaningful relationships that I am beyond grateful for.

I make a lot of money. I have had access to opportunities, resources, and people who have changed my life for the better.

And I've learned so much about myself along the way—things I would never have learned otherwise. I never would have redefined what success looks like for me if I hadn't traveled this exact path. I would never have understood what it takes to make this path satisfying and fulfilling.

But if I could go back and do one thing differently, it would be to change the way I experienced the path from the very start. I had so much more control over that experience than I realized.

So do you.

The definition of success that has been given to you was never meant to serve you. It was meant to serve someone else.

Not only does it not serve you, it doesn't serve the people around you. It doesn't serve the world.

It keeps you from recognizing your own worth and from understanding that you have an innate value that is not dependent on anything other than your existence.

It keeps you:

- ❖ From being yourself.
- ❖ From taking up space.
- ❖ From taking risks.
- ❖ From being creative.
- ❖ From finding what your truth is.
- ❖ From finding your genius.
- ❖ From being fulfilled.
- ❖ From changing your life.
- ❖ From changing the world.

I don't want that for you. I bet you don't want that for you either. You must define what success looks like for you. You decide how you want to experience this one beautiful life. That decision is yours and yours alone. You make the rules.

Unlearning the way you've defined success your entire life and deciding what it looks like for you isn't an easy process. It's scary. Messy. Hard. Uncomfortable. Confusing. Painful. Amorphous. Non-linear.

It requires you to get to know yourself in a way that you can't even currently fathom, to think about what you actually want in life. It requires audacity and a willingness to feel any emotion, even the ones that scare you the most.

But you know what else is hard? Living your life to meet someone else's definition of success and relying on that success to make you feel fulfilled.

Not only is it hard, it doesn't work. And ultimately, there is no amount of success, no matter how you define it, that will preclude you from being human and experiencing the full panoply of human emotions.

But you can experience them differently. You can experience more of the emotions you want. You can turn down the dial and frequency of your negative emotions. You can choose to experience the negative emotions that move you toward growth, instead of the ones that keep you stagnant. You can create a life that you want, one that is right for you.

You get to choose your "hard." Choose now. And choose intentionally. You are choosing either way. Stop putting off your own fulfillment.

The grass isn't greener on the other side. It's greener where you water it. Your life deserves to be watered now.

(Disclaimer: I don't actually know how to take care of grass. But I think you're probably supposed to water it.)

CHAPTER SIX

The Gift of Hope

by Rebecca Evans

> *"The life I imagined for myself wasn't out there. I had to create it. There was no roadmap because where I was going, there weren't any roads. ... It's up to you to decide where you're going, and how you're going to get there."*

MY PROFESSOR'S EYES WERE clear and steady. The statement took my breath away.

"You'll never be a constitutional lawyer."

It wasn't said cruelly, just matter-of-factly. My heart was pounding and my ears were ringing, as if all the oxygen had been sucked out of the room.

"But have you thought about family law?" she said, and then smiled. "You would be amazing at that."

I tasted bile and felt the old, familiar hand of dread squeezing my chest.

Family law.

She was right, of course. I would be a fantastic family lawyer. And people need someone like me—someone who would care about their cases and the little details of their lives, who would empathize when everything familiar and comforting starts to crumble around them and all they can see is the gaping hole left behind.

I was only halfway through the first semester of my 1L year of law school, but I already knew I wasn't going to become one of those people who would treat their clients as a job. Sure, I'd draw boundaries and create some separation; but when people trust me with the most intimate challenges of their lives, I care.

I looked around me and saw lawyers and doctors and therapists who had constructed proverbial walls to protect their emotions. It kept their hearts safe; yet some part of our humanity is lost when we distance ourselves from others that way.

We've all experienced it—the doctor who is behind on his or her rounds and just wants to check off the boxes as quickly as possible; or the attorney who only sees you as the billable hours he or she needs to maybe make partner by Christmas. Nobody wants to be treated like that. Sure, the doctor might prescribe to you the right medication—if he was even listening; but you leave dissatisfied, feeling unseen and unheard.

Despite the challenges that come with the legal profession, I decided to keep my humanity. I chose to keep caring, even though I knew some of what I would hear and see throughout my career would be traumatizing. I wanted my clients, my judges, and my colleagues to know that I care about them, about their circumstances, and about our profession. Being a lawyer is not just another job to me.

I appreciated what my professor was trying to do. She had evaluated my ability, my challenges, and my options; and even though it was a rapid assessment on her part, statistically speaking, she was right. I had virtually no chance of ever working in an appellate constitutional firm. Yet, I would have no problem finding work as a family lawyer.

Problem is … I knew it would kill me. More on this later.

EIGHT YEARS EARLIER, when I was a young mother with two small children, living in the suburbs outside of Dallas, I read about a nonprofit law firm that had a case going all the way to the U.S. Supreme Court. I had no legal training, but as I read the article, something inside me rose up and shouted. This was a cause worth fighting for! And they were doing it for free. I was in awe. I told my best friend that I would work with that firm someday—even if only as a volunteer.

I didn't know it at the time, but the lead attorney on that case, a former Supreme Court clerk, lived in my neighborhood and we attended the same church. I was teaching her children in my Sunday nursery class. I didn't know what my students' parents did for work, but I knew what the parents ate for lunch and what Daddy's favorite bad words are. I knew who sang songs with and read to their children and I knew exactly which lullaby would soothe each child.

I knew my neighbor was a wonderful mother who taught her children well. She clearly got things done. Her husband was just as smart, and was also the kind of guy all the toddlers would instinctively reach for when they needed comfort. That's all I knew about them; but really, what else do you need to know about people? I liked them a lot.

Years later, I left Texas to go to Utah. I was a single mom with three kids and no income. I needed to do more. I had that feeling again, that feeling that I needed to do something with my life. I decided to take the LSAT and apply for law school. I even wondered if I could volunteer for the firm I had seen in that article, so I looked it up.

That's when I realized who my former neighbor was. She was a genuine legal rockstar, a heavyweight in the ring I had the temerity to try to enter. Her husband was a former Supreme Court clerk and a notable attorney in his own right.

How is she doing it? I wondered. She seemed to have it all: work, family, the dream. What I had were many people telling me not to attend law school. They gave me several reasons:

"Your children will never see you. Is that the life you want for them?" they would say.

Or

"Is this so you can be rich? Finances won't bring happiness."

Or

"Why would you want to do that? Wait, have you heard the one about the attorney who walked into a bar?"

This woman was a practicing attorney, pursuing justice at the same time she changed diapers and made lunches and put her kids to bed at night. She had a happy family.

There's a way to do this, I realized. Success doesn't have to be working 60 hours a week in a lonely office while you miss your kids' milestones and cuddle up to your golf clubs for company.

Hope.

That's what I was feeling. Hope.

Hope that the life I had always wanted to design could actually be mine; that I could master my fate and make a difference in the world—even at the age of 35.

I sent this woman a Facebook message, suddenly feeling shy. She was a Supreme Court attorney, and I was no one. Well, I had taken care of her kids for a few hours every Sunday, but that was about it. Why should she care about me? Would she even respond?

I was ecstatic when I got the call. I asked her how she did it. I told her I wanted to go to law school and that I didn't know anything about how to be a lawyer, especially the kind of lawyer I wanted to be. I asked for a roadmap.

She gave me something better ... she gave me her support. She offered to answer any questions I had, and she agreed to write a letter of recommendation.

FLYING HIGH FROM MY acceptance to law school, I set my sights on working with that firm. I knew nothing about constitutional law, but I learned. I inhaled every article and book I could find. It was never enough. I felt like I was drinking out of a fire hose after being parched my entire life. I had never felt so alive. This was my purpose. This was what I was meant to become.

Now, statistically speaking, appellate constitutional attorneys are at the top of their class, having attended some of the best schools. They are picked for the best federal clerkships—even Supreme Court clerkships—and they are picked by the best appellate firms. What I wanted to do wasn't impossible—for someone at the top of her class.

But I wasn't at the top of my class.

With three children to care for, a new husband, and a baby on the way, I was the poster child for an exhausted student. I didn't have the hours to commit that some of my younger classmates did. My time was spoken for, long before I woke each morning. The only thing keeping me afloat was my remarkable ability to speed read and take accurate notes.

I wasn't flunking my classes, but being squarely in the middle had never inspired any federal judges as far as I had been able to determine. Yes, I researched it, first out of hope and later out of a morbid sense of despair.

My professor and career counselors were right. There was no way I was going to be a constitutional attorney.

But I went to a convention in Philadelphia anyway, where I knew attorneys from that firm would be. I brought my baby. And my notes. I raised my hand when a topic came up that I was passionate about, and I asked the questions and made the comments I ordinarily would have been too terrified to make.

Afterward, one of the attorneys from that firm came up to me and asked me who I was. He said I should apply for a clerkship with his firm. I thought the world had stopped spinning. After checking to make sure that gravity was still working and my feet were still on the ground, I told him cheerfully that although my grades weren't top of the class, I would love the chance to prove my worth.

For a minute, I thought he was going to tell me to give up. Instead, he gave me hope.

"You're absolutely worth it," he said. "You would be an incredible addition to our team. You already have what you need. We can train you in the rest."

I must have floated home because I don't remember the plane ride. I threw myself even more passionately into my constitutional studies. I joined a Supreme Court clinic and worked my way through one terrible brief after another. At first, it was confusing. Over time, I improved.

Unfortunately, I didn't do the clerkship with that firm. It broke my heart, but family circumstances changed and I couldn't even apply. For a while, I was my own worst critic. I saw the attorney again a few times, and he asked me why I hadn't applied. I gave a blithe response and we laughed. But inside, I died a little more each time.

Maybe I didn't deserve to be happy. Maybe I wasn't smart enough to design my own life.

Maybe I wasn't worth it, after all.

TIME PASSED. I did a clerkship with a local district judge and I stayed in the Supreme Court clinic, much to my professor's chagrin. When he asked me why I stayed, I told him.

I told him how I loved the Constitution and wanted to spend my life advocating for our rights. I told him how much I needed to learn, how it felt like I was breathing for the first time and had a purpose. I told him about the newspaper article and my friend, and how I knew, deep down, this was what I should do with my life.

And this man, this former Supreme Court clerk with decades of impressive cases, accolades, and experience that I didn't have and might never have, looked at me with tears in his eyes and said:

"You're in the right place. But you'll never make money as an appellate attorney. There's not a lot in it. Most of us made our money elsewhere."

Suddenly, he was talking pragmatically about how to make my dream come true.

"Do business litigation," he said. "Do that first. That's how I made enough money to do this. A few big cases, and I could focus on constitutional law."

And he walked away, smiling and shaking his head. I had an ally.

Graduation day came. I made it, and I walked that stage with my diploma in hand and tears streaming down my cheeks. Only a few people knew how hard law school had been for me and what I had been through, or how much it hurt knowing that I could have been top of my class:

❖ If I hadn't had a family to care for.

❖ If my mother-in-law hadn't had terminal cancer.

❖ If I hadn't had a baby my first year.

❖ If there hadn't been a lawsuit.

❖ If my health had been better.

❖ If I'd only had a few more hours a week.

I had no job prospects. I felt worthless. But I never once considered practicing family law. My own trauma with family law ran deep. I knew I wouldn't be able to separate my client's trauma from my own. Maybe I could at first, but after a while, I would want a break from it all. I didn't want to be the jaded attorney. I wanted to care. And caring would break my heart. I could see it, as clearly as I could the letters of each job application I filled out.

My epitaph would read:

Here lies Rebecca Evans. Attorney. Worked late nights every week taking care of her clients. Tirelessly gave of herself in service to the community. Died at 42 of heart failure.

That just couldn't be my story; so family law was still out of the question.

I got a clerkship with two district court trial judges in my state, and I loved it. I loved the variety, I loved the intensity, and I loved the challenge. I learned what good writing looked like in the wild, and I heard everything the attorneys said when the judge left the room. I learned exactly what kind of attorney I didn't want to be, and how to be the kind of attorney that others respect even when they sit on the other side of the table.

Most importantly, I learned how to process the terrible things I'd hear and see every day. I learned how to care without letting it consume me. I learned how to give generously without depleting my own emotional tanks.

And I learned that my income wasn't enough to support my family. So back to the résumés and applications I went.

THIS TIME, I HUSTLED HARD. I landed a job interview with a guy who wanted an attorney to do Telephone Consumer Protection Act (TCPA) claims. I had no idea what TCPA claims were, but I found out. Turns out he wanted someone to sue spammers. That sounded good to me! I did the interview.

Somehow, I ended up getting an offer to be the Chief Legal Officer and Managing Partner of a new legal-tech firm. I negotiated a decent salary and equity package, and I dove right in. I was busy interviewing and hiring staff and attorneys, creating all the litigation documents we would need, and figuring out exactly how the law worked for telemarketing violations. I built a fully remote law firm, with associates and paralegals all over the nation. I worked from home; and together, my partner and I built a practice that put our employees and clients first, building in efficiency and creating sustainable profits in a radically different way than any traditional law firm had done.

Within a few months, it was clear that we needed to expand. We needed counsel in every state. I didn't know anything about practicing law in multiple jurisdictions, so I asked a lot of questions and did a lot of reading. We could practice in every state as long as we complied with their licensing regulations, set by the state bars of the various jurisdictions. That was not a problem—for 41 states. The other nine had rules prohibiting law firms from operating under "fictitious or trade names." You had to have a law firm that was named after a managing partner (and it didn't have to be a person currently living either).

In order to operate nationally, I would need to persuade nine state bars to change their rules. We tried asking nicely. Twice. They ignored our letters.

So one day, after months of intense daily preparation and sleepless nights at my computer, I gave the team the go ahead. I supervised and directed while amazing local counsel in each of the nine states simultaneously filed complaints in federal court challenging the constitutionality of these prohibitions on trade names for law firms. As far as I've been able to tell, no one had ever filed lawsuits against nine state bars in different jurisdictions on the same day before. It was a colossal feat; there were a few hiccups along the way, but we did it.

That day, the voices in my head were of all the people who had told me not to go to law school, that I would not be able to have a family and a practice, and that I would never be a constitutional appellate lawyer. I also remembered the people who believed in me and told me I was worth it ... that I could build the life I wanted.

This pivotal moment marked the start of the kind of practice that made my heart sing, in the best tradition of a total geek: my practice in constitutional law, appellate litigation, mass torts, and multi-district litigation began with those first terrifying steps, after years of heartbreaking (but steady) preparation.

THE LIFE I IMAGINED for myself wasn't out there. I had to create it. There was no roadmap because where I was going, there weren't any roads.

No one can design a life for you. No one can tell you what success looks like for you, because they aren't you. They can only show you the road they've chosen. It's up to you to decide where you're going, and how you're going to get there.

There are bumps along the way, and tears, and pain.

But there are also people who will give you the priceless gift of hope. They will cheer you on. They won't tell you which path to follow because they don't know. But they will walk with you for some of that path, and they will leave their light behind to help you see your own path more clearly.

Someday, if you stay true to your core values and you refuse to quit, you will find a way. You will find your way. Sometimes we just have to fail our way to success—whatever that looks like for us.

I was not in the top of my class. But I am a constitutional appellate attorney and a dang good litigator.

By the way, we won those nine constitutional suits.

CHAPTER SEVEN

My Net Worth

by Bhavna Fatnani

"Penning this chapter has been one of many fantastic opportunities that have allowed me to pause and reflect on my experiences. The joy of sharing my story with the world surpasses any fear or hesitation of allowing others to have a glimpse into my life."

LET ME TELL YOU A STORY, a story of a little girl who was the apple of her parents' eyes and the life of her house.

Being the youngest member of a close-knit nuclear family in India, I was the most pampered person in the house. But with all the love and pampering, there were many restrictions placed on me for protection. My parents didn't intend to restrict my progress; but the strong influence of society made them establish stricter rules for me than my elder brother.

Having faced differential and preferential treatment, I always wished to strive for equality. Even as a child, I would dream about a world where the rules were the same for all. And since everything big starts small at home, I decided to stand up for myself. I decided to share my thoughts with my parents about striking equality in employment choices, going out with friends, or moving out of my parents' home.

"If my brother is allowed, why not me?" I would say. My father always lovingly responded, "That's how society is, my dear. It is not because I don't want you to fly high; I'm afraid society would cut your wings."

Over time, my rebellious differences and my parents' supporting actions helped strike a balance at home. My parents' mindset evolved. They began trusting my decisions more than fearing the anti-social elements of society. They are now my most prominent critics and biggest cheerleaders, letting me fly as high as I wish! I can proudly flaunt to the world that my parents are change-makers in our society. They were willing to see their child happy even when they knew she was making a mistake but confident that she would be learning alongside.

TO LET YOU IN ON a secret, I was an introvert and barely had any friends as a young girl. If you had known me then and continue to know me now, you'd scream with joy looking at how much I've changed.

It was college life that changed me. Behind all the unintended sibling rivalry was the hidden fascination with my brother's traits. He was my opposite. I looked up to my brother and wished I was as fun and communicative as he is. He is everyone's favourite; and the little girl in me wanted to be just like him. He was my role model.

In college, I followed in his footsteps by joining a committee (of which he was a part of previously) where we organized intra- and intercollegiate events. This helped me open up, as I had to interact and coordinate with multiple stakeholders. It was my first step in developing leadership skills.

I started off as a member and moved up to be the president of the committee. This was a significant achievement for me. Initially, people recognized me because they had known my brother; but within two years, I had created my own identity.

I realized during this period that I enjoyed interacting with people. I would put my heart and soul into projects, and I was blessed with a team that did the same.

Along with this role at college, I was preparing for the Company Secretaryship (Chartered Secretary) course. Attending tuitions, managing the sponsor meetings for events, coordinating the approvals from the authorities—all done to the best of my ability. I was learning a critical life skill—delegation.

Looking back, I think it would have taken me less time to complete the course had I delegated some of my responsibilities to other members. But because of the inherent fear of not getting the perfect outcome, I ended up controlling how the work was carried out. Fast forward to today, I do not keep a tab on how things are done. All that matters is that the work is done well and the results are met. I lend support but I do not micromanage the process.

While I was completing all the exams to be qualified as a Company Secretary, I also underwent the 15-month mandatory internship. This internship was my second breakthrough.

LIKE MOST OF US, I had received multiple rejections and had been ghosted for many opportunities I had applied for. Then a friend of mine casually asked if I was looking for an internship opportunity. She had received an offer from a firm of one of the renowned Practicing Company Secretaries. She recommended me to the recruiter at the firm. I was called for the interview the next day.

Referrals and recommendations have played a significant role in my life. It was only because of my friend's suggestion that I landed such a great opportunity. I gave the interview, cleared the final round, and was asked to join the very next day. Things couldn't have gotten better than this, I thought.

But life had other plans. While I was hoping to work and manage a large clientele at the firm, the firm's partners had recommended me to one of their premier clients. I was being outsourced to manage a client that was a global leader in financial services. I was on Cloud Nine when my interview was successful and knowledge transfer had been initiated.

I was asked to work from the client site and report to the Vice President (Legal) for the work I was entrusted with. The knowledge transfer continued for a few weeks at the client site. This was the time when I found another role model—my reporting manager, the Vice President (Legal).

After the transition was completed, I was all on my own, coordinating directly with the legal team under the guidance of my reporting manager. With his help, I learned effective technical skills and how a manager is supposed to be. If I may say, he indeed set the benchmark high.

He is an ideal boss. He is my self-proclaimed mentor. Even after seven years, I recall all his learnings, loud and clear. He stood up for me when I was right, guided and corrected me when I was wrong. Every time I was asked to step up and manage people in life, I would remember how he managed the team and matched the skills.

He made me a confident legal professional. It was his suggestion that led me to pursue my formal legal studies. He encouraged my interests in legal drafting even when it was outside the scope of the assignment. I can never thank him enough for being my role model in the ruthless corporate world. He made it all seem easy and authentic.

I then moved to pursue my full-time legal studies while interning with an independent law practitioner. A friend's referral worked wonders for me and helped me land the interview. By happenstance, I was interviewing at two places the same day, one after the other. However, after the first interview at the law office, I was asked to immediately start working. I couldn't believe it. "This was it!" I thought to myself.

I worked with the team at the law office for six months, and to date, I cherish the relationships we formed. I visited them a few times at the law office and participated in their personal celebrations. I bonded with a colleague so well that I even received an invitation to her hometown.

After six months of internship at the law office, where I learned nuances of legal practice, it was time to make the next switch. It was time to learn about the hot subject of intellectual property rights.

You wouldn't be surprised if I told you it was another friend's referral again, which got me the internship at the new firm, would you?

Relationships are the best earning a human can make! Time and again, my network has proven to be my net worth. Thank you to all who have helped me.

I learned the technical skills, made some new friends, and then it was time for the next big jump. It was time for a full-time legal role.

HAVING CLEARED MULTIPLE rounds of interviews, to my surprise, I got the confirmation call from the recruiter while I was on vacation with my friends. After a relaxing holiday on the beach, I was energized and excited for the next big moment in my career, albeit a little nervous.

This role was perfect for enhancing my legal skills and making the most of the previously possessed technical skills. I was a part of the team that drafted and filed corporate law lawsuits, the specialty being oppression and mismanagement cases.

The rebel awoke in me, and we gave our best to help the clients with their legal rights. The partner at the firm still calls me a "rebel child at work." Being ever hungry for knowledge, I was happy to be seated around senior team members. They were not only supportive of me but always helped me work effectively in relaxed surroundings.

Having become an ambivert, I was quick to make friends in the office. But we bonded beyond work. We kept each other's mental health in check. We suggested regular breaks, took charge of additional unplanned work, and even coordinated each other's tasks.

Considering my performance and the plan for revamping the existing team, I was entrusted with managing a new team and a new profile of work—contract drafting and negotiations. And, all of this happened in less than 12 months of being associated with the firm.

This wasn't the first time I had worked with contracts. I had previously worked with contracts during the mandatory internship. I had also assisted my team member in times of crisis with proofreading and editing. Seniors around quickly noticed my command of the language and the keen interest to learn more about contracts.

This led to my team winning all assignments for contract drafting and negotiations. I managed to outperform myself by reviewing new drafts each time while entrusting another team member with critical drafting tasks at hand. After all, I had learned delegation was important. With the appreciation flowing in, I ensured my team member received his due credit for the hard work he had put in. And, I must admit, he always had ideas to improve drafting skills.

But soon after making my team independent and self-reliant, it was time to bid goodbye to this fantastic team and fly higher. It was time to move seven seas away to Toronto, Canada. But before that, there was a small, much-needed break in store for me.

I took this period to rest and to spend time with family, time that I had lost initially because of the strict deadlines at work. I needed to relax. I went on vacations with family and made enough memories to be able to survive away from home.

A VERY DEAR FRIEND had suggested moving to Canada for a better work-life balance and growth in the legal experience. Following that advice, I applied for a permanent residency (PR) visa. However, the timelines were massively impacted by the number of applications.

As I had a minimum of six months on the estimated timeline before my PR would be approved, I decided to pursue a contractual role. I explored and learned about packaging and labeling requirements for FMCG products during this stint. Again, this was for one of the company's biggest clients, and I was entrusted to manage the deliverables independently. My manager was highly supportive and always there when I would get stuck. Big shout out to her! I wouldn't be where I am today if it hadn't been for her.

Just when my contract with the company was about to end, I was offered an extension. But with the excitement of leaving the country soon, I let it go and decided to consider the time off as a break to prepare for the next adventure in life.

The anxiety during the end of the estimated timeline was extreme because many people were suggesting that the approvals could be delayed. On the other hand, I had quit the job that could have possibly jumpstarted my career for the long run.

I woke up in the middle of my sleep and happened to check my email. Guess what? I had received the email from IRCC, the authority for granting approvals for visa applications of Canada, stating my visa application was approved and I should submit my passport for stamping. Woohoo!

Ever since I was a child, I had wanted to follow in my brother's footsteps (my brother was living in London at the time), but now it was time for me to take a big step for myself—to bid farewell to my nest. I was happy to have made this decision but equally sad to be away from my parents.

I did not know how or what I would do when I landed. I only had a few college acquaintances who were landing around the same time. It was a brave move but I did not feel the stress of this change. I was ready.

On the other hand, my parents were in a happy-sad state. Remember, I was the protected one? They held back their tears until I boarded my first ever international flight. Every time after when I would call from Toronto, I would see a slight tear in their eye. Maybe they did miss me much. Or perhaps it was a change they weren't ready for. Oh boy, you can never correctly guess a parent's emotion, can you?

I LIVED NINE MONTHS in Toronto, trying to make my way into the legal industry. I managed to do odd jobs for a few months, but I was disheartened as I faced trouble getting hired in the legal sector. The reason for the struggle was not a lack of skills. It was the lack of local work experience. Transferrable skills were not given much consideration even by some employers who promised "inclusiveness and non-discrimination" at their workplace.

I was frustrated and did not know what to do next. Never had I felt so lost. I sought help from some of the legal professionals with whom I had come to know through study groups. Unfortunately, we were all facing the same problems as internationally trained lawyers. They suggested actively networking within the legal community to get some guidance from others who had been through a similar phase and had established themselves in the industry.

All the excitement I had before the take-off had fizzled out. Rejections, ghosting by recruiters, feeling alone, being away from home, failing an exam—it was all chipping away my self-confidence. It felt like I had no strength to continue the fight.

Before losing all hope, I resumed connecting with industry experts through LinkedIn. In one of the coffee chats I attended, a lawyer asked me what my passion was. I was numb. I had no answer. I had been working 12 to 14 hours but never thought this would be something that would matter.

Meanwhile, for more than three years, I had been actively contributing articles to an e-newspaper that was India's first women's only newspaper. Frustrated with the legal job market, I decided to offer freelance writing services, taking my writing skills a notch higher. I was approached by a Canadian lawyer who wanted my help with blog writing for a fee.

My father would always say to me, "Good things take time to come your way, but they eventually do!" We quickly negotiated the terms, and I started ghost-writing blogs for him. Tips and tricks for drafting legal documents and writing articles came in handy. This was one good opportunity that came my way after a very long, disappointing period.

When that project ended, I had to shift my focus to exams that were required for licensing in Toronto. I decided to study from the comfort of my home in India.

When I arrived in India, my parents were so excited to see me. We did all the catching up—late-night movies, family dinner—and I had missed those relaxing head massages Mom always gave me.

While I was home, my father was also required to undergo minor surgery. Though not a major surgery, we were all very nervous. I did not have the heart to leave him while he was still recovering. Just when my departure was near, news about COVID-19 broke. It felt like the universe was telling me to stay. So, I did.

I HAD SEEN THE HARSH reality of the corporate world and had made up my mind to come out of my cocoon at all costs. I had to regain my confidence. I was not inclined to take up a job in India because my heart and mind were still in Toronto. My writing was my escape from the mental chaos. Thus, I began the journey of writing posts and connecting with legal professionals regularly on LinkedIn.

"Could writing be what I am passionate about?" I asked myself. I certainly enjoyed doing it. I decided to reach out to my friends to ask if anyone needed help with short-term content writing projects. I started my freelancing journey with the help of a good friend whom I knew through college and the committee I was a part of. A referral worked its magic yet again. My friend took a chance on me. We worked on multiple projects together in a short period.

As a freelancer, my first job was guest blogging for a start-up. I wrote three trending posts in just a short time smashing the LinkedIn algorithm! One day, I was approached by a lawyer in the UAE to write blogs for his firm. Woah! It was serendipity. I was back in the legal industry, even if indirectly.

Over time, I worked with clients based in the UAE, UK, India, and Canada. Though the income was not stable or as much as a full-time job, I was happy. I was content. But you know what they say: The universe always has something better in store.

I had managed to keep in touch with the manager at my last job in India, where I learned about the packaging and labeling requirements for FMCG products. In fact, we even had a catch-up with former colleagues at the client site just before the pandemic broke out. One evening, she called to ask if I was open to a full-time job. The job was at the same "Big Four" accounting firm with which the business division had previously merged.

And there it was, right before me. A referral from my previous manager could land me a well-paying legal job, a new profile that would help me grow and learn in the comfort of my home.

Without a second thought I said, "Yes." The referral landed me an interview. I appeared and got shortlisted, negotiated the package, and was onboarded. I guess all the good karma decided to come back!

FAST FORWARD TO 2021: I am completing a year in the above role. I've been outsourced to one of the premier clients, managing the deliverables independently. I have met yet another person who has become my unclaimed, unannounced mentor. He was the project manager for this particular project I was being staffed on. He guided me on how to think instead of what to think. And for this, I shall forever be grateful.

Apart from my full-time role, I set aside time to guide lawyers and law students who wish to move to Canada to further their legal careers. I'm still pursuing the exams for accreditation, though it feels like a task to be studying after long work hours. I guess the "human" me wants to limit the "superhuman" me from doing it all at the same time!

I am part of a state council that educates and empowers women in areas concerning wellness—financial, mental, emotional, and spiritual, among others. Believe it or not, I came across this opportunity through the communication group created by the publisher of the e-newspaper I previously contributed to.

In my free time, I collaborate and write guest blogs on various topics. My interest is leaning toward health and wellness. You can find my LinkedIn posts using #HerstorieswithBhavna. This hashtag has evolved after multiple rounds of discussions with friends and family. Similarly, I managed to secure a domain name and build my personal website. It is www.iBhavna.com.

My heart still wishes to move back to Canada in the hope of exploring other scenic regions, especially Vancouver. I now aim for a work-life balance, where I have time to pursue my passion and spend time with family. After all, they are my rock-solid support system. I often remind myself not to mindlessly chase money and fame in the pursuit of being successful in the corporate rat race.

Penning this chapter has been one of many fantastic opportunities that have allowed me to pause and reflect on my experiences.

The joy of sharing my story with the world surpasses any fear or hesitation of allowing others to have a glimpse into my life.

CHAPTER EIGHT

I Simply Asked

by Pat Gillette

"Although I wanted to be "perfect" in everything I did, I learned quickly that I couldn't be. No one can. And the sooner you realize that, the closer to perfect you will become. Because striving for the "P" holds you back, it precludes you from trying new things, and it makes you doubt yourself. So accept that you will never feel that you are performing at 100% in your personal or professional life. Be satisfied with probably being 95%!"

TWO SONS. NOT SERIAL KILLERS. One husband. Forty-seven years. Big Rainmaker in BigLaw. Firm Leader in BigLaw. Successful trial lawyer. Elected community leader. Member of several nonprofit boards. Speaker and author on a national circuit.

That's me. I am not special. Nor am I a superwoman. And that is why I want to share my story with others. You may not do what I have done, but you will be surprised at all you can accomplish with a few tips.

I grew up in South Central Los Angeles. I was one of two white kids in my senior class—but I became student body president. I was raised by parents who taught me that anything was possible; and I believed that. My high school gave me insight into what it feels like to be a minority, except that I knew as soon as I went 10 miles in any direction, I would be back in the majority. But that experience imbued me with a passion to fight for civil rights and to try to correct the inequities I witnessed in my community.

As I entered college, I decided I would become a politician who would be devoted to making change and having an impact. But that dream was dashed as I got active in politics and realized I wasn't cut out for that kind of gamesmanship. So I did what I thought would be the next best thing—I decided to become a lawyer.

There were no role models for lawyers in my family of Lebanese and German immigrants to this country. While I and all my siblings went to college and graduate school, each of us was inventing it as we went along without any real guideposts—other than my parents' constant encouragement to pursue whatever path we wanted and to never give up. So my older sister got a master's in science, my brother got an MBA, my younger sister got a PhD in education, and I got a law degree.

WHEN I GRADUATED, my goal was to be a plaintiff's employment lawyer so I could advocate for the civil rights of minorities and women. Unfortunately, there were no jobs in plaintiffs' firms for new lawyers. So I ended up going to a large management labor and employment firm (38 lawyers was "large" for such firms in 1976) and stayed there for two years. I justified my joining the "dark side" as I began to realize that the partners who worked with our big clients had far more influence on corporate policy and culture than any plaintiff's lawyer could ever have. That reality carried me through and proved to be true for the rest of my career.

At that firm, I turned down "union busting work" early on because I didn't believe in it. So I got myself onto the litigation team. How? I simply asked. The team was small, as discrimination and wrongful termination cases were just beginning to be filed with any regularity. Most of my colleagues and peers didn't consider this to be "real" labor and employment work, but I thought it was going to be the future and I wanted in on it.

I was right.

In 1978, I left that firm to go in-house at Bank of America. I did not make that decision because I had kids (I didn't) or because I wanted a different life style. I chose to leave because I wanted to see how businesses operate from the inside and because the culture at that first firm was not consistent with what I wanted out of my career. So I took a risk and went in-house.

Why was that a risk? Because BigLaw viewed in-house lawyers as second-class citizens and it was highly unusual for a second-year lawyer to go in-house voluntarily! But I didn't really care what people thought, and going in-house turned out to be one of the best decisions I have made over the course of my career.

THE PERSONNEL LAW ADVICE section of Bank of America was a small but important part of our 200-person legal department because the employment-related lawsuits that were filed or threatened to be filed often required us to meet with some of the highest-level executives in the company. We litigated all our cases ourselves, seeking outside counsel only for non-litigation matters. As a result, I got a lot of opportunities I never would have had if I had stayed in private practice. It was exciting and terrifying—like being taken to the top of a snow-covered hill and told to ski down without any skiing experience!

But I survived and thrived.

In fact, this in-house experience was a turning point in my career. Not only did I get to try a bunch of cases, argue substantive motions, handle appeals, develop bank-wide policies, introduce creative and impactful programs to address inequities in the workplace, and present to and interact with executives, I also learned how to think like a business person instead of a lawyer.

I knew that my job was to understand the business objectives of my in-house clients and find a legal way to allow them to realize those objectives. (Basically, that means finding a way to say yes instead of no—unless something is illegal.) That was driven home by our General Counsel, George Coombe, who required every lawyer in our legal department to work in the bank branches (which at the time were the "heart" of all banking activities) for two weeks so that we would understand the core business of the company.

From that experience, I learned that to give good legal advice, you have to know the business of your client. That became a guiding principle for me for the rest of my career and, in my opinion, is what helped me become a major rainmaker in my firms.

WHILE AT THE BANK, I had my first son. It was 1982 and there was no such thing as paid maternity leave and certainly no paternity leave. Nevertheless, I was allowed to take six months off (unpaid) following the birth. And when I returned to work, my husband and I quickly realized that we had to be a team. My husband was a highly accomplished appellate lawyer working for the California Attorney General's office (and ultimately Kamala Harris's Chief Deputy of the Criminal Division). He and I divided household responsibilities—although not evenly—but more than before we had kids. We approached family life as a team. We had a full-time nanny who came in at 8:00 am and left at 5:30 pm when my husband got home. I usually got home after 6:00 pm.

There were certain ground rules that we held hard and fast with both of us working full time. First, I love to cook—it's how I relax. So I made sure I was home every night to make dinner for us as a family. I quickly learned that we were in charge of defining "normal" in our household, so it was "normal" to eat dinner at 7:00 or 7:30 pm.[5] Every night, we would all sit down for dinner together and talk about school, work, friends, challenges, and joys. Dinner time was communication time.

Second, weekends were sacrosanct. Sure, certain tasks had to be done—grocery shopping, laundry, house projects, baking cookies for the next week of lunches—but our kids did those things with us, so we didn't lose precious time together. Sundays were reserved for family time—hikes, baseball games, swimming, beach time, or just fun games and kid projects around the house.

Third, vacations were a must and they were family events. We took the kids to Europe, Asia, across the United States, and up and down California. Our vacations were always at least two weeks (sometimes longer). And we were "unplugged"—which was much easier since there were no cell phones, no texts, and no emails for most of the time our kids were growing up.

Fourth, holidays and birthdays were big events. For example, we often started planning birthday parties six months before the event, creating themed parties that ranged from pirate extravaganzas to Mission Impossible. And because there was no Pinterest, no books on themed parties, no roadmap for how to do themed birthdays, we had to create the games, the cake, the invitations, and the

---

[5] As a result, when our kids went to college, they called home to express their shock that people would even consider having dinner before 6:00 pm.

ambiance. Looking back on it, we were a little nuts. But it was fun to be creative together.

Fifth, my husband and I made time to be part of our kids' lives. We signed up for field trips and then told judges and bosses we were "unavailable" on those days. We took our kids to swim class and told our colleagues we had an "appointment" at 2:00 pm every Wednesday. We volunteered to be on the board of trustees for our kids' schools, to take on discreet tasks for school events, to coach soccer on the weekends, among other things. If we missed work time, we made up for it after the kids went to bed. Yes, we were a bit sleep deprived, but we enjoyed every moment. From dinner time through bedtime (which for our kids was usually 9:00 pm), we were focused only on them.

AFTER THREE YEARS as one of the lawyers in the bank's Personnel Law Section, my boss left and I was made the head of that section. I stayed in that position, managing three other lawyers and a paralegal. But, in 1984, before the birth of my second kid, I decided to return to private practice—a small boutique firm specializing in labor and employment. Why did I leave? Because the new head of Human Resources at the bank did not value lawyers. As a result, the highly effective and collegial team of lawyers and human resource professionals was replaced by distrust and dysfunction. I couldn't see myself staying and simply dealing with that.

To my surprise, the reputation I had developed at the bank resulted in almost every bank in California sending me their litigation, including all the Bank of America litigation for Northern California. Bank of America had never allowed in-house attorneys to take bank work with them as they left the legal department.

How did I get them to allow me to do that? I simply asked.

In this small boutique firm, I again learned invaluable skills. Vic Schachter, the best mentor I have ever had, was the chair of the firm. He taught me everything I needed to know about marketing:

- ❖ How to listen actively to clients and potential clients;

- ❖ How to think about ways to make a client look good;

- ❖ How to be creative, innovative, and strategic; and

- ❖ How to find ways to differentiate myself from other people.

There was no person too low in the hierarchy to be a potential client; there was no event that wasn't an opportunity to develop a client. He made client development an everyday experience and defied the traditional mantra that business development is hard, or involves golf, or is something only men can do. Vic taught me how to be a trusted advisor to my clients by looking out for them and building long-lasting relationships that would survive challenges from other attorneys who were good but didn't understand that relationships were as important as reputations.

I loved my experience at this boutique firm. But after six years, when I began to see a change in the culture at the firm that I thought might destroy the collegiality, I started to look elsewhere. I had a big book of business at the time, so my options were plentiful.

I landed at Heller Ehrman and there I stayed for 17 years. I became a practice group leader—one of the few women to hold that position. I was appointed to the Policy Committee—the executive leadership team for the firm. I headed up the Women's Initiative.

How did I get those opportunities? I simply asked.

I also continued to be a major rainmaker and thus joined the ranks of the highest paid shareholders in the firm. And I began to speak out nationally on gender issues that I thought were plaguing the legal industry.

IN 2006, I FORMED the Opt-In Project with a young woman, Anne Mercogliano, from whom I would learn a great deal. She was a recent college graduate with a passion for women's rights. We convinced Heller to allow us to study how corporations were retaining and advancing women within their ranks to determine if we could apply those principles to the legal industry.

How did I convince my firm to let me do this project and provide funding? I simply asked.

Over that year, we held conferences in various cities across the country, focusing on different types of business models: professional services, financial services, tech, government, and academia. From those conferences, we developed best practices for advancing and retaining women, and then wrote the Opt-In Report that took those practices and imagined how they could be applied to law firms and legal departments.

The report was immediately recognized nationally, in large part because it discussed "women's issues" outside of the traditional context of "work-life balance." This report was about the systemic and structural barriers that were keeping women from succeeding in the legal industry. It was a new take on an old problem. It was different, interesting, and it challenged traditional norms. It was pretty radical.

The Opt-In Project catapulted me into the national scene on women's issues. I was asked to speak all over the country on the results of the study. That gave me the opportunity to seek out chances to speak and write about other issues holding women back in law firms and corporate legal departments. Before I knew it, I was one of the most sought-after speakers on these issues; was appointed to the ABA Commission on Women in the Profession (mostly due to one of my best friends and mentors, Roberta Liebenberg); and I was writing for prestigious journals, newspapers, and other publications.

I was having a great time in a firm that I loved, continuing to grow my business so that I remained a major rainmaker in my firm, and filling my "extra time" with the issue I was most passionate about—the advancement and retention of women in the legal industry.

AT THE END OF 2007, however, the culture of my beloved Heller Ehrman began to transform with a change in our leadership. I felt like this firm that I thought of as my family—even though we were hundreds of attorneys across the country and internationally—was imploding. I tried to change the direction of the firm, but I couldn't. So, I took my team—lawyers and paralegals—and went to Orrick, Herrington and Sutcliffe.

While at Orrick, I participated in the 2016 Hackathon run by the Diversity Lab. My incredible team came up with the idea for the Mansfield Rule, which requires firms to have at least 30% of their candidates for leadership positions be women or minorities. Although we didn't win the competition for the best idea, we won the larger prize, as the Diversity Lab (under the amazing leadership of Caren Ulrich Stacy) took our idea and transformed it into one of the most impactful actions law firms and corporations can use to change the face of leadership in law firms and legal departments.

After eight years at Orrick, and after finishing leading a team on one of the most interesting and challenging cases I had ever handled, I decided to leave. My associates who had come with me from Heller were settled and protected. I had set up the transition of my clients to other lawyers. I had initiated and completed a data-driven study of what makes rainmakers successful, and I had published a book called Rainmakers: Born or Bred, based on that study. Now, I wanted to spend more time spreading the word about the findings of that study to actively dash some of the myths about what it takes to be a rainmaker—particularly for women.

When I really thought about what made me happy, I realized that I wanted to spend the next part of my career doing what I felt passionate about—speaking and writing on how to advance and retain women and minorities in the legal industry.

Out of the blue, I got a call from JAMS asking me to be a mediator for employment cases. I thought it would be a good way to keep my brain active. So I agreed with intention of making mediation a sideshow to my speaking and writing. But I soon gained a reputation, due in large part to the support of plaintiffs' lawyers, as an effective mediator. The balance of my work began to tip toward mediations.

Today, I have finally found a way to balance my passion for speaking and writing with my passion for mediating cases. I do both, working harder in some ways than I did as a litigator but enjoying every bit of it.

I AM REALLY NOT SPECIAL.

It may seem as you read this that I have accomplished a lot. But that was over a 40-year span and at a time when the legal profession wasn't nearly as intense as it is now. However, the five basic principles that allowed me to have a successful professional and personal life have not changed:

1.   Ask for what you want.

Many of the opportunities that presented themselves simply came to me because I asked. I learned early on that—for most of us—if you don't ask for opportunities, you won't get them. And what is the worst thing that can happen if you ask for something you want? Sure, someone might say "no." But when I hear "no," I hear "not now." This applies to professional and personal opportunities. If you don't ask your partner for help, you may not get it. So ask. If you don't ask to be put on a trial or a deal, someone else will. So ask. If you don't take risks by putting yourself, your expertise, or your reputation on the line, you will not grow. So ask.

2.   Find a mentor.

Mentors and sponsors have been very important over the course of my career. For my professional mentors, however, I didn't seek out people based on gender. In fact, during my tenure in BigLaw, "queen bees" were prevalent and they often tried to keep other women from being successful. I looked for mentors with whom I felt comfortable and whom I felt cared about me, without regard to what they looked like.

I had many mentors over my career: a highly successful male plaintiff's lawyer; a male in-house counsel who had a ton of jury trial experience; and a woman who was my peer in a corporation but who was wise beyond her years in terms of how to manage difficult political situations at work. My best sponsors were high-level leaders in my firms who I "courted" by being helpful to them, by supporting them and offering to advance their initiatives. And they, in return, championed me and wanted me to be part of their leadership teams.

I also had mentors in my personal life—mostly women—who helped steady me on the balancing beam known as "the working mom." There weren't many women who worked and had children, so finding someone who could understand the tremendous guilt (and joy) associated with being a working mom was hard yet essential. Those women are still among my best friends.

3. Keep your priorities straight.

My family was always my priority. Trying to maintain that and a high-powered litigator career, however, was always a challenge. But if the balance had to be tipped, it was always tipped in favor of my family. As far as I'm concerned, my sons are my greatest achievement in my life. They are enlightened, socially responsible young men who are compassionate, generous, and caring adults. They are as different as night and day—one with a PhD in mathematics and the other with a master's in public policy. But at their core, they are the same—committed to family, to community, and to each other.

I also kept my priorities straight at work. As is obvious from my story, the culture of the places I worked was as important as the work I was doing. I refused to work in an environment that I felt was inconsistent with my values and expectations. So I made some hard choices. But when you spend most of your day hours on the job, I think you have to believe in the work you are doing as well as the people with whom you work.

4. Get rid of perfect.

Perfect. This concept dooms so many women. Although I wanted to be "perfect" in everything I did, I learned quickly that I couldn't be. No one can. And the sooner you realize that, the closer to perfect you will become. Because striving for the "P" holds you back, it precludes you from trying new things, and it makes you doubt yourself. So accept that you will never feel that you are performing at 100% in your personal or professional life. Be satisfied with probably being 95%!

5.   Be gracious, generous, and genuine.

It is important, especially for women, to be able to promote yourself and your abilities, to be able to talk with confidence about what you have achieved and your skill sets. But it is equally important to think about those around you—your colleagues, your clients, your friends and your family—and find ways to put their interests on par with yours. Find ways to help others. Give back to your professional and personal communities.

What goes around comes around.

So this is me and what my life as a lawyer and a mom have been like. There were times when I felt overwhelmed, exhausted, inadequate, and like a failure in all aspects of my life. There were times when I felt tremendous guilt about my kids, my husband, and my career (I still do at times). But all of this evens out over time. And the joy that comes from doing what you love, personally and professionally, cannot be matched.

I am glad I am a mom. I am glad I am a lawyer. I hope some of what I have shared will help you find your own path to joy and happiness.

CHAPTER NINE

Why Not Me?

by Zeynep Goral

"Even now, I struggle to embrace "being successful" despite all the metrics confirming my success. By all accounts, I'm an independent businesswoman earning a sustainable living as a writer. Occasionally, I catch myself owning everything I've accomplished, and it's happening more often."

IT TOOK ME 10 YEARS after passing the bar to find my footing in the legal industry. And somehow, ironically, I ended up coming right back around to where I started.

The difference is, this time, I am my own boss. I set my own definition of success. I forge my own path; and the way forward is clearer than it's ever been.

I haven't always been so confident in where I stand.

When I first worked as a summer associate, I used my background in web design and marketing to advocate for a revamp of the firm's website. Over several months, and between working on client cases, I rewrote all the website content—from the practice area pages to the attorney profiles. Most of the text had originally been written by the attorneys, themselves.

Immediately, I saw the drawbacks of "writing like a lawyer" online—long blocks of text, case names, statute numbers, and dates. Let's not forget the detailed legal analyses of court opinions. All the attributes that make lawyers good at what they do, unfortunately, did not translate well when it came to client-facing content—especially online.

I stepped in to bridge that divide between legal speak and lay-man's terms.

Even though I was there as a summer law associate, I looked forward to the web content work every day. Any legal work started to feel like an interruption.

Fast-forward to post-graduation, I became a lawyer when the market crashed in 2010. I didn't practice at all the first four years I held my license, relying on my previous skills for work. When I did land a job in law, I went into the document review trenches—first with foreign language projects that paid quite well. When that well ran dry, I started taking English projects that didn't pay nearly enough to survive, even with as much overtime as I could muster.

Meanwhile, the work dragged me down. Document review presents few paths for advancement unless you want to become a project manager. Projects could end without warning or notice. The downtown commute left me exhausted by the time I returned home every day. One of my biggest monthly bills was daycare for my dog. (I'm a millennial, what can I say?)

By the end, I was staring at nearly a thousand documents per day, 10–12 hours straight, six days per week, in a room shoulder-to-shoulder with 24 other people—you know, the legal industry's version of hell? (It really gives Danté a run for his money.)

IN LATE 2018, a friend of mine created and released an online course about how to start and run a copywriting business. It piqued my interest but it was hundreds of dollars and I was skeptical. I'd never bought into an online course over $50 before, but I got to see just how hard she'd worked on this one. Still, I let the first enrollment period pass me by.

In early 2019, she opened enrollment again. It had been four months and I was still in the same place—hating document review and dreaming of something better. I took the plunge. I bought the course even though the price had gone up by 50%.

It changed my life.

For the next three months, I worked through each of the modules in the course. The first two lessons were all about mindset, another term that made me skeptical at first. Soon, I realized that the mindset sections were probably the most valuable part of the course—and there's a heck of a lot of value in the rest, so that's saying something:

- ❖ I learned how to shift my thinking from an employee mindset to a business owner mindset.

- ❖ I learned to properly value my time and my work product.

- ❖ I learned how to set my price on my terms.

- ❖ I learned to set boundaries with work hours that serve me.

- ❖ I learned how to cultivate relationships with clients who saw my value.

I've gone back through the mindset work multiple times. I plan to go back again, as I now stand between all the original goals I've accomplished and what lies ahead.

Another part of the course involves picking a niche to focus on. Obviously, I chose the law. I had specialized knowledge because I was a lawyer. I'd actually written content for law firms before; I'd just never realized that it could become a career. My web design and online marketing background gave me a strong foundation in search engine optimization.

Once in a law firm interview during law school, a partner gave up on interviewing me altogether (I was clearly not a fit for BigLaw in any sense and I couldn't fake it, either) and started giving me advice on my résumé. According to him, my skills made me appear to be a "Jill" of all trades—web design, online marketing, writing, and being a lawyer. He saw this as a negative.

He was right, after all. I didn't quite fit, at least not the way I presented myself. But copywriting brought all my skills together. It fit. I fit. And it feels good.

I DEDICATED MYSELF to my copywriting business full-time in May 2019 when my last document review project ended. I started turning down any further projects from that point on. I earned back the price of the course within a few months.

But as the months went by, I "cold" emailed a thousand potential clients and booked no more than a dozen. I had some work but not enough to cover my bills. About a year in, I remember thinking, "I've never worked so hard on anything before in my life" (and I've taken the California bar exam twice!). Unfortunately, I didn't know what I was going to do if this didn't work.

Six months later, my business hit an inflection point where the effort became a little more effortless. All the hard work I had put in up to that moment converged and bloomed at once.

First, I wrote a couple of successful case studies that got a decent amount of attention, one of them based on the work I had done with my first client who still works with me today. Second, I found the place that my target clients like to hang out (turns out, lawyers love LinkedIn). And third, another client referred me to my biggest client yet. Since then, I haven't had to do any client outreach. All of my recent client inquiries have come to me.

One of my clients even tried to hire me full-time but I didn't let the conversation get far. Although the road here was tough, I wouldn't change where I am now for anything.

IN JANUARY 2021, I made 10 times what I had made in January 2020. Two months later, my business made the most ever in a month. Every month after that, I have made more than the month before. In September 2021, I reached the monthly income goal I had set for the year—three months early and without the white-knuckled hustle that characterized the first year of my business. Simply put, my clients are happy and they keep coming back for more.

I crushed some personal goals, too. I'd always wanted a house with a yard for my pup to live out her golden years. (Again: I'm a millennial.) I made that dream come true with the money I earned from my business. I currently set my own work hours, which usually come out to less than 40 per week. I can even give myself a raise when I want one.

Sometimes, it seems surreal. How is this my life?

Part of the mindset work of the copywriting course involved unpacking my relationship with success:

❖ Why do I feel like I don't deserve success on my terms?

❖ Why do I feel like all my dreams are destined to remain dreams, never to be realized?

Even now, I struggle to embrace "being successful" despite all the metrics confirming my success. By all accounts, I'm an independent businesswoman earning a sustainable living as a writer. Part of me is constantly wondering when the other shoe will drop—surely something will happen to make all this crumble around me.

How dare I actually support myself with something that I enjoy!

How dare I be happy!

But as Mindy Kaling once asked: Why not me?

Occasionally, I catch myself owning everything I've accomplished, and it's happening more often. A friend and I started talking about Facebook advertising campaigns at a social gathering recently. Another friend asked us how we got on the topic. My friend replied, "I work in advertising." I replied, effortlessly, "I run a business."

CERTAINLY, MY SUCCESS looks different than what my parents had envisioned for me—a long and stable career in a single field where I would rise up the ranks in accordance with my seniority and skill over the years. That's what they did. The immigrant cliché was also strong in my family: the "doctor, lawyer, or engineer" creed runs deep. Guess which one of the three was the most appealing to me?

Recently, my dad exclaimed over the phone, "I guess this means I have a small business owner as a daughter!" We didn't buck the American dream after all.

But now the prompt has changed. Before, I was trying to survive. Now, I must learn to scale.

I currently have so much work I can barely keep up, and I love my clients. Over the last two years, I've not only earned more but I've gotten better at my craft. At first, writing a 1,000-word blog post would take me two days. Now, I can do that in a single afternoon.

My work is meaningful to me. I get to translate legalese so that non-lawyers can understand their rights. I help lawyers reach the clients who need them. Sometimes my friends have legal questions and I can point them to an article I wrote answering their question. I get to actually use all my professional skills to offer a unique angle of expertise.

Where do I go from here? About a year ago, I subcontracted some work to another writer. That project didn't go quite as planned (it derailed spectacularly), so the idea of hiring out more work fills me with trepidation. But part of me knows that contracting out work to other writers will be a step I'll have to take to grow. After all, what am I to do if I go on a vacation?

It's hard to trust the quality of my work to someone else, and hiring a contractor is just that. But businesses rarely grow on their own. And the help would be nice.

Speaking of vacation, I'm actually writing this on a weeklong family vacation at a beach house. I'm working full days all week long and testing my productivity on the road for the first time. I always work best with two monitors—one for research and the other for the document I'm writing. So I've figured out how to use my iPad as a second monitor next to my laptop.

ONE OF THE BIGGEST selling points of the copywriting business course I took was freedom—the freedom to set my own hours and rates, to pick my own clients, and to work from wherever in the world I'd like. Once the world makes it to the other side of the pandemic, I'd like to take advantage of that. Travel a few times per year, and write and work from wherever I go.

I also want to write more for myself, especially fiction.

Finally, I want to use my law degree to volunteer my time for causes I care about. This is the piece of my vision that reaches beyond just me—it's the legacy I want to leave behind.

MY PATH WAS NO get-rich-quick scheme. It took months of hustle and grind to get good traction. For a while, I wondered if I would use my law degree at all. But I actualized the life I wanted for myself, and my success gives me greater confidence in my next venture. In fact, the entire process of building my business was a series of small wins that helped offset the losses and it demonstrated my own power to myself—the power to change my circumstances to my will.

Now, that's a definition of success I can live with.

CHAPTER TEN

Choices We Make

by Tatia Gordon-Troy

"People ask me all the time if I regret not practicing law. My response is always the same. "No." That's because I found the path that truly fits me, and I still get to use the skills I gained from law school. Law school taught me more about myself than I think I could ever have learned on my own. It set me on a path I never expected to take."

THIS IS MEANT TO BE a success story. But it's really a story about self-reflection. Without self-reflection, how do we know when we've truly found success? This story is about asking the hard questions and finding the courage to answer them:

❖ Am I proud of what I've become and where I am in my life?

❖ Would I have done anything differently?

❖ Is this where I truly want to be at this stage in my life?

❖ Do I feel appreciated at work?

❖ What would I be doing if money wasn't an option?

I am an attorney, a writer, an editor, a publisher, a mom of a 20-year-old son, a soon-to-be divorcee, and a woman who is working on finding herself while building a business, two things I never really thought I'd have the opportunity to do—that is, the business and the self-reflection.

But let's first take a trip down memory lane. Like many of you, I allowed my workplace to dictate my life, weighted down by the "self-inflicted" guilt trip that accompanied my desire to leave work at a reasonable time in order to do things for myself or my family, such as exercise or attend at least one of my son's baseball games during a season. I say "self-inflicted" because no one on the executive level of my workplace would ever admit to instilling and/or instigating such a "you-don't-deserve-a-life-outside-of-work" culture. By the same token, they did nothing to convince us otherwise.

I talked myself into staying longer hours day after day because I felt I was making a difference. I felt it was expected of me as a member of the executive staff. I spent year after year, trying to prove myself or show that I deserved to keep the position I already had earned through hard work and long hours. I believed that I'd be recognized for my loyalty and devotion—maybe a higher raise or another promotion. I figured the more hours I put in the more money I would make for my employer, so it would be worth it in the end.

Eight years later, several pounds heavier, and too many premature gray hairs to count, I realized that all I had to show for my efforts was nothing more than what everyone else had received—notwithstanding the number of hours worked or any perceived return on investment from my time and effort. In fact, some of my colleagues seemed to fare better even while performing less and managing to "do it all" between the hours of 9 and 5.

All the while, I had missed out on memorable moments of my then 13-year-old son's life. I had justified my absence during his early years with my relentless ambition; for at that time, I was striving for a seat at the executive table. Nothing was going to get in the way of that. There were many nights when I would say goodnight to my son by phone from the confines of my office some 60 miles away because I knew he'd be asleep by the time I arrived home. "Mommy, why can't you be home to put me to bed? When are you coming home?" He would ask.

As he got older, he'd tell me to come to his room upon my arrival just so we could spend a few minutes together. Oftentimes, a few minutes would turn into an hour and my husband would get upset because this would disrupt our son's sleep. He was absolutely right, but when would there be any mommy and son time otherwise? Sometimes, we'd end up playing games and just talking. I felt guilty keeping him up late but I enjoyed our time together. After a while, my husband gave up, especially after our son started middle school.

I've always seen myself as the one who would make it to the top of any workplace in which I settled; and if I wasn't headed upward, then I was off to the next place with the same intent. I put off becoming a mother for the first nine years of my marriage. I truly thought it would send me spiraling downward in my career. Finally, I took the leap; but when I returned after four months of leave, I felt I needed to work even harder to prove myself; I had to make up for lost time. Ambition is a jealous lover in so many ways; this meant that I would choose to miss out on many major moments in my young son's life.

The desire to prove ourselves worthy of recognition fueled by our ambitions allows us to ignore the other important things in our lives, which leads eventually to unhappiness and burnout. We all deserve a better work-life balance.

NOW ENTERS THE SELF-REFLECTION. When big changes happen in your life, it forces you to pause and think about how you got to where you are and where you'd like to go from there. It's like a huge stop sign at a fork in the road. I was on the job for 15 years, I'd made huge strides and millions of dollars for this organization, and suddenly, all that changed. I'd become a victim of downsizing, rash decision-making at its finest. I was a 49-year-old woman who was at the top of her game, ambitious as anyone, and suddenly unemployed. My marriage was failing and my mother was suffering from dementia. It was like the perfect storm in so many ways.

I was faced with jumping back on that hamster wheel to find that next executive who would hold my life in his or her hands, or move forward on my own. So what did I do? I brokered a deal with the person who had just fired me to outsource my department's work to me. I did that because I knew she had no clue how many pending contracts there were floating around. But I did. That work kept me going for the first year while I made connections and landed my first client. That's when it hit me that maybe I was on to something.

I decided to start my business because I wanted to be there for my son and his milestones. I was committed to attending every baseball game to witness firsthand the homeruns and RBIs, to see him catch those fly balls, and to see him act as relief pitcher. In his last year of high school, he decided to run track, and I attended every track meet to cheer him on. Having my own business allowed me to do that.

I was also able to be present for my mother, who was wasting away before my eyes. Within months of my termination, her dementia had progressed and she was unable to care for herself. The following March, she was gone. I held her hand as she slipped away. But for the grace of God and my choice to forge my own path, I would not have been there for her when she needed me most.

For three years, my family never knew I had been let go; I had essentially replaced my job with my own business.

WHEN I WENT TO law school, I was thinking I'd practice law. Duh, isn't that what law school is for? Of course, all I knew about the law was what I had seen on television—shows like *Perry Mason*, *LA Law*, *Matlock*, and *Law & Order*. I didn't realize I had an interest in writing until I went to law school. While there, I felt compelled to write op/eds. for the school newspaper; one in particular involved the right to counsel and competent representation. Never before had I felt comfortable publicly sharing my opinion and I actually enjoyed doing it. It was the positive reaction received from those I respected that made me realize I might have something going for me.

During my 2L year, we were enthralled by the OJ Simpson trial, which was televised. I watched with enthusiasm the legal analysts who gathered each day to discuss the day's happenings in court. I looked at them and said, "I can do that." Before I knew it, I had enrolled in journalism courses at another university while still maintaining my full-time law student status.

Instead of landing internships with local law firms, I was interviewing at the local news stations and getting hired—the perfect place to learn how to be a TV journalist. After graduation, I headed to New York to interview with the hottest station on the air at the time—Court TV. I couldn't contain my excitement when I was offered an associate producer spot on staff. That excitement waned quickly when I was told the salary. Meager doesn't quite describe it. I couldn't justify the move to New York and certainly couldn't see how I would afford a daily commute. Not to mention, I had recently married and it didn't quite seem to be the right time to start a long-distance marriage. With my proverbial tail between my legs, I returned to Baltimore feeling dejected. I quickly pivoted to print journalism and worked for three years as a reporter and editor for a legal newspaper.

Opportunities continued to present themselves. As a reporter, I met and interviewed Congressman Elijah Cummings who then offered me the press secretary job in his D.C. congressional office. I was responsible for writing his speeches, op/eds., press releases, email newsletters, reports, surveys—you name it, I probably wrote it. There was never a dull moment, as the job pretty much consumed my life. He was a junior congressman at the time and needed to prove his worth to his constituents and to his congressional colleagues. I am proud to have played a small role in the building of his legacy.

SOON AFTER LEAVING the halls of Congress, I went to work for a small general practice firm where I focused on employment and administrative law. It was the perfect setting—three partners and me. I was their first and only associate.

While attending law school, I had reached the conclusion that law practice wasn't quite the right fit for me. But I had always felt pressured to at least attempt to use my degree for what it was meant for. When I decided to dip my toe into the water, I purposely joined a small practice so that I would experience as much as I could.

From day one, I was preparing cases, researching the law (the traditional way, in a library, of course), writing motions and complaints, interviewing clients, traveling to and from court, tracking down witnesses, examining and cross-examining witnesses on the stand, helping to *voir dire* jurors, and playing an integral role in the representation of the firm's clientele.

Although I was pretty good at spotting issues and thinking of ways to resolve problems, I grew tired of it quickly. Notwithstanding the thrill that accompanies an occasional win, much of the work was tedious. I grew to despise the adversarial nature of the profession and the one-upmanship that permeates it. It was draining, both mentally and physically. I assumed the bulldog, pitbull, or piranha personality as often as needed, wondering whether there would come a day when I wouldn't need to expend so much energy.

I also hated the slow and methodical movement of the halls of justice—it was like watching grass grow. I was dismayed every time clients were forced to drop their cases simply because their pockets weren't as deep as the other side's.

I simply couldn't see myself spending the next 25 years practicing law. The faces might change, but the process stays the same. It truly was a great experience and I managed to choose a firm with some of the best partners anyone could work with. They were more than bosses, they were mentors.

But my creative juices were bubbling and telling me to move on. I was missing my community of creative writers and news reporters; so when an editor position in Washington, D.C., opened up, I jumped at the opportunity. I had no idea I would spend 15 years there, but I was consistently moving up the ladder and being recognized for my worth, while experiencing one accomplishment after another. I worked my way up to the C-suite, earning a seat at the table.

EVERY STEP I'VE TAKEN and every job I've held have helped me hone my writing skills. I've had the opportunity to write in countless styles—from the standpoint of laying out a case to the standpoint of laying out a book marketing campaign. I've also had the pleasure of being a storyteller for my clients. Whether it was laying out the facts for an EEOC complaint, writing a speech to engage and inform local constituents, breaking down the gist of a U.S. Supreme Court case for the news, or ghostwriting a chapter for a book, writing has been at the core of my career success. I owe my success to the education I received and the enlightenment I experienced in law school.

People talk down about law school—"it's boring, it's tedious, it's hard, it's complicated, we hate the Socratic Method," etc. And, sure, I probably have said the same things. But what law school did for me was bring out the person I never knew existed—the one who not only has an opinion but isn't afraid to voice that opinion and to join the conversation. You see, I grew up a very shy child and I am an introvert by nature. I started to find my voice in college, but law school truly made me feel confident enough to speak on any topic, to command any room, to believe that I deserve to occupy a coveted seat at the executive table.

Had I not gone to law school, I'd still be in some small cubicle in a corporate office somewhere crunching numbers. I worked my way through college in a small accounting department within a large insurance company. I'd planned to get an MBA or CPA. No offense to CPAs but I was bored with that lifestyle, yet I thought it made the most sense. Then a relative of mine suggested law school. I would never have gone into journalism had it not been for law school. It gave me direction by showing me what was possible, by giving me the confidence to believe that I could do anything, and it gave me the gumption to go after whatever I set my sights on.

As an introvert, I learned how to bring forth my inner extrovert. I became the person I believe I always should have been. Law school was my "mic drop" moment.

People ask me all the time if I regret not practicing law. My response is always the same. "No." That's because I found the path that truly fits me, and I still get to use the skills I gained from law school. Law school taught me more about myself than I think I could ever have learned on my own. It set me on a path I never expected to take. In my publishing business, I work with attorneys all the time and I get to talk shop with them without having to be the one writing the motions and arguing the facts.

NOW, TO ANSWER THOSE questions I posed at the beginning:

Am I proud of what I've become and where I am in life?

Yes, I am. I have followed the path I believed was the right one for me and I have accomplished so much, both personally and professionally. I have used my skills and experience to help others reach their goals. I don't do what I do to receive recognition, but it's nice when I do. Will I continue on this path? You never know. I think that's the beauty of having a law degree and a background in media, communications, journalism, and marketing. My skills are in demand across many industries; however, right now, I am enjoying being my own boss.

Would I have done anything differently?

I often wonder how far I could've gone in TV journalism had I accepted the associate producer positon at Court TV. I really wanted to be in front of the camera and that position would've been a huge stepping stone. But there's no reason why I can't pursue my passion for TV journalism with the numerous outlets at my disposal. A colleague of mine and I are currently developing a podcast that will debut in 2022 and I'm toying with the idea of starting a YouTube show dedicated to covering the stories behind the headlines. Time is my only enemy at this point.

Is this where I truly want to be at this stage in my life?

Though I never thought I would ever have been terminated from a place I had dedicated 15 years of my life to, I actually appreciated it because it gave me the push I needed to do something I had always wanted to do—become an entrepreneur. And although running and building a business is no walk in the park, I wouldn't change this experience for the world.

Do I feel appreciated at work?

This is an interesting question when posed to a one-person shop owner. I am the CEO, the accountant, the secretary, the social media specialist, as well as the editor, writer, and publisher. I have a cadre of highly experienced freelancers with whom I have built strong, trusting relationships and whom I can count on to work with me on publishing projects. My clients appreciate me and what I do for them.

What would I be doing if money wasn't an option?

I would volunteer my time to teach young people writing skills that can open more doors for them in the workforce. Many high school and college students struggle with their writing. Having good communications skills is imperative to success, and I would love to lend my experience to the cause.

I DON'T EXPECT OTHERS to follow in my footsteps. My path is somewhat unique, and yours will be as well. You must find happiness and satisfaction in life on your own terms.

Remember, you are in charge of your own destiny. Go for what you want, what you desire, and be prepared to step outside your comfort zone to achieve your goals.

Believe in yourself and take ownership of your future.

CHAPTER ELEVEN

Out of Love

by Angela Han

> *"When I started doing more things out of love, I started looking at the reasons I love my job, even when it feels menial. I started serving my coaching clients out of love. When I asked for help from family, I was doing it out of love for them because I was making time for the things that stimulated me so that I could be more present for them."*

"MEDIOCRE" IS THE WORD I was always the most afraid of. Growing up, my mother instilled in me a desire, a need to be the best at everything—whatever I chose to do. I would always strive to be at the top of my class, to be accepted into the top universities, to land the most competitive and prestigious jobs. When I couldn't be the best I'd feel like such a failure. My mom would tell me, "It takes time to be the best," but I wouldn't listen. I just wanted to bring honor to the family as fast as I could.

We all tend to be very selective about what we want to hear, and that becomes part of our conditioning. I conditioned myself to believe that I must be perfect at all times, and I know this resonates with a lot of you. You always find it in yourself to strive for the best and be the best for the people around you.

But striving to be the best at everything comes with a price. We work so hard to get so far in our lives, and we realize one day that something doesn't feel right. Everything has seemed so perfect until this point, at least on paper, yet your feeling tells you otherwise.

I am here to tell you to listen to that feeling, because that feeling is everything.

It is your intuition.

Let me tell you how I went from total strangers to best friends with my own intuition.

I WAS IN THE middle of law school when I experienced a breakthrough—a moment when I looked up from my mess. I was bulimic and falling behind in class. I had no motivation, and I was resentful of the entire institution. There was a handful of good friends who always managed to bring a smile to my face, but I focused more on the imperfect parts of my life—the people who left my study group, the professors who didn't care, the firms who rejected me. I prioritized the people who didn't give a sh*t about me, and I allowed those people to define my worth. That left me miserable.

I had finally had enough of letting hate and resentment govern every part of my life. In that moment, I saw that I was the last person I was prioritizing. I knew I needed to decide how I was going to live my life moving forward—whether I was going to continue this pattern of self-hate and allow others to define me or cut myself a break and start over. I needed to get to know myself. I needed to place myself first. I needed to figure out what makes me happy.

At first, I didn't know how to accomplish this. It had been too long since I was actually curious about who I am. I had forgotten how to get in touch with myself.

I decided to focus on something that everyone seemed to be talking about—finding one's passion. At the time, I hadn't quite gotten out of the conditioning that I should follow everyone else's path, so I Googled the meaning of passion. A YouTube video by Evan Carmichael popped up, and he said something about how we can find our passion in our biggest pain. That was a unique concept to me, so I decided to try it.

MY BIGGEST PAIN was feeling like I didn't belong. I had come to the United States on my own as an immigrant to attend college. That is when the bulimia started. Seven years later, during my first year of marriage, I finally began to feel a change in my spirit, an inner voice telling me that I was ready to move on from that phase of my life. During this time, I had turned my attention to exercise. I could see how much stronger I was becoming, physically, which then led me to become stronger mentally and emotionally.

Seeing myself go through the external and internal transformation through exercise was such a meaningful experience for me. Without realizing it, I had become passionate about exercise, passionate about feeling healthy and confident, and passionate about life. I felt I needed to share what I had learned with others, so I started teaching other people how to accomplish the same through exercise.

I started as a personal trainer for about a year, then transitioned to health coaching for another year, and finally moved into life coaching.

Finding my passion allowed me to channel my biggest pain into something positive and helpful for others. Let's face it … at the end of the day, our greatest desire is to make a meaningful difference in the world. Where most people get stuck is on figuring out for themselves how to make a difference and how to make that difference meaningful. The key is to decide what is meaningful to you; then use that to make a difference in other people's lives.

What is meaningful to you will be different from what is meaningful to someone else. There is no right or wrong answer. When we remember that we are the most powerful person in our own lives, the "right answer" rarely matters. Our bodies and our souls are constantly giving us the answers we need. At some point, the answer for me was exercise and becoming a personal trainer at a local gym. The pandemic then shifted my location but not my passion. I began training people online. Life will find a way, and that is the beauty of life. It is truly an adventure, and you get to decide what ride you will get on next.

WHILE I WAS BUILDING my side business, I was also growing as a lawyer. I started my law career and my side passion right after passing the bar. People ask me how I am able to accomplish both at the same time. It's as if doing more than one thing diminishes your capacity to be successful at either.

We tend to fall victim to the limitations that other people impose on us. If we do anything outside of being a lawyer, it must mean that we are not competent as lawyers. I have heard this plenty of times.

I asked myself if that really was true for me. But the only way I could answer it, to know for sure, was to actually do the things I wanted to do and find out.

I don't want to give you the impression that juggling a law career while building a side business was easy. It wasn't. When I was trying to create my own website and began putting myself out there, I had absolutely no idea what I was doing. But I went back to the spirit of my business, the spirit of my career, and the spirit of my life, and what it was telling me was that I couldn't just stop there.

If you're thinking, "What the heck is this spirit that you are talking about?" listen closely. It's the voice that is telling you something is right or something is wrong. It's your intuition. And if you're thinking, "I have no idea if I am listening to my intuition or my fears," here's the biggest difference: Intuition feels like you are positively expanding your energy, while fear makes you feel like you're negatively expending your energy.

At one point, I started feeling dismayed and disappointed at how poorly my business was doing. When it came to the question of whether I should quit when it felt the hardest, I looked at my options. Honestly, none of the options available felt expansive to me. I just felt like I was stuck in a rut, losing money, and gaining no traction with my podcast. But the answer was easier when I asked myself which option felt like I was expending energy. That's when I realized that if I quit my business, I would be in permanent misery, wondering "what could have been" had I continued on despite the roadblocks.

Oftentimes, we become so accustomed to the idea of expending our energy on things that don't really matter. We convince ourselves that this is "what we should be doing," that we "genuinely can't do the things we want to do." But when we allow ourselves to question our own motives, we generally find our way to the truth.

After being rejected by more than 200 employers following graduation from law school in 2017, and finally landing a position that paid me a salary in the bottom quartile, I knew I had to create something of my own. We tend to attach our value, worth, and identity to our profession. But I knew that attaching my worth to my profession as a lawyer was unsustainable because a job is something that can be taken away from me at any point. I wanted to focus on something that no one could take away from me, something I could call my own.

EARLIER THIS YEAR, my toddler suffered from severe burns by tipping over a boiling pot of soup that I had placed on the table. She had to be rushed to the emergency room. I was devastated. I felt guilt and shame like I had never felt before. Every time I look at her scars, I think about how I had caused this to happen and the feeling is painful for me.

Then someone told me that my ambition took away from time with my family and was the reason my toddler had the accident that got her admitted to the emergency room. I struggled with this because I believed it was true. But instead of trying to dismiss it with thoughts like "that is nonsense" or "just snap out of it," I decided to honor my thoughts and feelings. I accepted them as part of who I am.

Looking at her suffer but also seeing her coming back to life through her unbelievable resilience, all I could think about was how much I loved her and how I did not need anything else to survive.

Whether I was present enough before, I created space for myself to reevaluate how I was showing up as a human being. Were my values aligned with who I was as a person? Did I like the mother that I saw in myself? Did I like the wife that I saw in myself?

I approached those questions with curiosity instead of judgment. When I did, I found that I had an infinite capacity to love. I realized I was more present out of love. I was able to draw boundaries out of love. I was able to balance work and home out of love.

Looking back at my career and my business, the most memorable moments were the times when I closed a deal out of pure love for the customer or when I completed a project out of love for the company's mission. Those were the feelings that sustained me and made me feel alive.

When my decisions started to come from love and not fear, I stopped doing things out of obligation. I stopped hustling. The majority of the revenue from my business came when I actively worked less and made more time for the things and the people I love.

There is nothing that will look so good on paper yet come with no heartache and heartbreak. On each of our journeys, we will experience that lump in our throat or that sinking feeling in our stomach. But the sooner we decide to honor each of those uncomfortable feelings as part of who we are, the sooner we get to shine in our humanity so that we can love others more and serve others better.

STOP THINKING THAT once you reach a certain point in your career, perform a certain act, or receive a certain recognition, you will be who you want to be. Too often, we think we need to have a certain job or live at a certain place or be with certain people in order to be happy. But how many times does that actually work the way it sounds? How many times have you gone after things that you thought would make you happy, yet it didn't quite free you the way you thought it would?

I thought that being a lawyer, and growing a successful business, was going to help me be a happier person. It turns out that being the person I want to be—someone who loves, someone who is free—is why I have accomplished so much in my life.

Who are you being? Are you loving, kind, free, independent? What feels right to you?

When I started doing more things out of love, I started looking at the reasons I love my job, even when it feels menial. I started serving my coaching clients out of love. When I asked for help from family, I was doing it out of love for them because I was making time for the things that stimulated me so that I could be more present for them.

I have become comfortable in my own skin—as a lawyer, a mother, a wife, and an entrepreneur.

IN REALITY, I will always have moments where I feel silly and stupid. There have been plenty of moments in my life as a lawyer when I have thought to myself, "Wow, I can't believe I don't know this." There are moments with my family where I think to myself, "I could have been more loving to my husband at that moment." There are moments in my business where I think, "Didn't I make that same mistake yesterday?"

We will always make mistakes, and we will continue to learn from them. I mean, would you rather be standing on the mountain top with absolutely nowhere else to go?

Life is about constant progress—new ideas, new movement, new concepts. It's what makes us feel alive. Your missteps and your mistakes are simply an indicator that you are on your way to something even more exciting.

When I think back to when my mom would tell me to strive to be the best at whatever I chose to do, I now understand what she meant. I have spent too long trying to be "better" than others, to beat the competition; and in doing so, I lost myself.

My mom meant that I am already the best at what I do because there will never be another me.

There will never be another you.

When we recognize the unparalleled power in our own uniqueness, there is no other conclusion.

CHAPTER TWELVE

Not My Father's Dream

by Talar Herculian Coursey

"My family immigrated to the United States for "the American Dream"; but it wasn't until my father's death that I realized I was living his dream and not mine. At 35, I dared to dream for myself for the first time in my life."

MY FATHER SPENT several months out of the year in our home in Lebanon after retiring. In 2006, he fell ill and was stranded after war broke out between Hezbollah and Israel. By the grace of God, I made it to him in the Bekaa Valley of Lebanon from California 12 hours before he died.

When I arrived in Lebanon, I spent several hours with him, listening to George Straight. We talked very little, as it was difficult for him to breathe. But with the little breath he had, he made sure that I would pay his debts in town; then he asked whether I had made partner yet at the firm.

I had not.

Success has had different meanings throughout the different seasons of my life. But I never really defined success for myself until recently. I remember my parents defining success for me dating back to the fifth grade at Dhahran Academy in Saudi Arabia. After appearing in a school play as Marc Antony in Julius Caesar, I decided I wanted to be an actress. But my father shot that down real quick.

He told me to do something that would give me a steady paycheck. So I decided I would become a teacher, like him. But that wasn't good enough. My father had been a teacher for over 30 years, traveling all over the world, and felt that it was a thankless job that didn't pay well.

He was finally satisfied when I told him I planned to become a lawyer. He told me that as a lawyer, I will still get to act while collecting a steady paycheck.

I STARTED MY legal career as a file clerk at Fisher Phillips, a national labor and employment law firm. I worked there while attending the University of California, Irvine (UCI), just down the street from the firm.

But UCI wasn't my choice; it was my father's choice. I wanted to attend UCLA. One of my most rebellious acts of defiance as a teenager was applying to UCLA behind my father's back. I wanted to attend UCLA after high school, but my father had other plans. He insisted I go to UCI because it was closer to home. I begrudgingly acquiesced. He wasn't paying for college, but as an obedient immigrant child, I couldn't imagine going against his wishes. I didn't want to make another concession, but I couldn't convince him to change his mind.

After graduating from UCI with an English degree, I headed for San Francisco's UC Hastings, College of the Law. Three years later, as I was about to graduate, I still had no job lined up. Luckily, I'm the persistent type; I was able to leverage my network to land my first job practicing employment law with a small insurance defense law firm. My training consisted of "sink or swim." I've always been a good swimmer, so I swam.

My parents were forced into retirement shortly after I graduated from law school and my brother and I began supporting them. My meager pay at the insurance defense firm was not enough to pay student loans and support my parents, so I started looking for another job.

I contacted my mentor at Fisher Phillips and told him that I wanted to make a move. I didn't intend to return to Fisher Phillips because I felt that I would still be regarded as "the file clerk." He convinced me that wouldn't be the case and then invited me to return as an associate. Five years later, three months after my father died, I made partner at the firm.

MY FAMILY IMMIGRATED to the United States for "the American Dream"; but it wasn't until my father's death that I realized I was living his dream and not mine. At 35, I dared to dream for myself for the first time in my life.

When an opportunity arose to join one of my clients, Vista Ford Lincoln, as its first General Counsel, I walked away from Fisher Phillips. In doing so, I took a pay cut, traded in my house in Southern California for a condo in Salt Lake City and traded in my Lexus for a Ford. Ten years later, I have never been happier.

Admittedly, the thought of leaving crossed my mind recently when a much larger dealer group offered me a position that seemed better in terms of long-term stability. The group consisted of 30 dealerships across six states compared to the two dealerships under Vista Ford Lincoln. It even came with a significantly higher salary, a "corner office" in a high rise, and the prestige of working for a large company.

What intrigued me most about the position was the potential for long-term stability. I was very open about my plans with my employer. They were very understanding, but they also didn't want me to leave. I then received the assurance I needed to convince me to stay—ownership. You can't get more stable than that! For all intents and purposes, it was a "win-win" for both of us.

I have it all and have succeeded as far as I'm concerned. I have a wonderful job as the "Chief Problem Solver" for bosses who are my best friends, and whom I get to talk to daily while getting paid for it.

IN THE LAST few years, I have come to the realization that, like your spouse, your employer cannot fulfill all your "needs." Sometimes you need to complement your life with other activities and relationships to increase life's satisfaction.

With the flexibility that my job offers, I pursue both creative and philanthropic projects. I recently became a published author: *#Networked* and *Ralphy's Rules for Living the Good Life* (both available on Amazon with all profits going to charity). I run the Salt Lake City Half Marathon every year to raise money for the Society for Orphaned Armenian Relief. I am a founder for "Sisters in Law" and "LinkedIn for Lawyers" on Clubhouse. And if that weren't enough, I am a real estate investor and a certified yoga instructor. Lawyers really can be multifaceted.

I have a blended family with four amazing boys and an employer that allows me to make them a priority. And, of course, I have a dog—Jackson Johnson Herculian Coursey—my "furrapist."

I am successful based on what I value the most; and I am so very grateful.

CHAPTER THIRTEEN

Pathway to Healing

by Marta Keller

> *"The behavior of the claimants and my own experiences with secondary traumatic stress, combined with the inability to truly feel better and the "yoyoing" between feeling lost and scared to grasping for direction and purpose throughout my life, suddenly made sense to me."*

FOR MOST OF MY LIFE, I didn't know how to be with the ever-present and often subtle messages of my body. They came in the form of sensations, feelings, thoughts, and images. They ebbed and flowed in the most supportive ways. Yet, I didn't always notice them. Even if I did, I didn't understand them, especially when their persistent nature compounded to an intensity that became unhelpful. So, I often ignored them and pushed through. I couldn't even share with others what was happening in my body or mind. I was afraid of being judged.

My inability to be with the messages of my body is how I ended up in law school. The defining moment leading to that decision was when the flame that had been ignited within me for so long to become a bestselling fiction author suddenly died out.

For years in my youth, it was the opposite. I sat in front of an old desktop computer in the cool basement or with pen and paper in the sunny kitchen, writing for hours. It was an effortless process for me to shape the latest images and ideas that arose in my mind into short stories, poems, and even 100-page manuscripts. I was inspired by the multiple books I devoured within days regardless of their length.

I loved that there was no limit to where one could take a reader through fiction. Everything and anything was possible and it felt expansive in my body. I shared snippets of my work with great enthusiasm with others, including publishers. Their resonance and support of my storytelling fueled my passion to keep writing.

Then I went to university, and it was like a bucket of cold water had been dumped on my creativity. I suddenly felt the pressure of being an adult—held to a higher standard within a rigid system while needing to figure out exactly what I wanted to do with my life.

English classes didn't captivate me anymore with their rigorous analysis and tedious essays. Reading classics left me restless and frustrated, as their formal language was difficult for me. My fire went out completely after taking a creative writing class. I was struggling with agonizing writer's block. I felt self-conscious with my incapacity to write stories with ease as I once had. I anxiously questioned my identity as a writer. I lost belief and trust in myself. By the end of the first year, I stopped writing.

IF I WASN'T A FICTION WRITER anymore, I didn't know who I was or what I wanted anymore. I didn't dare share my internal anguish with anyone. I was too humiliated. The only thing I knew for sure was that I felt constant pressure from my parents to succeed at school. So even though I felt ashamed that the one thing I was supposed to be good at, the one thing I had dreamed of becoming, the one thing that had been meaningful, and the one thing that was no longer an option for me, I still needed to excel. As I was excelling in biological and environmental sciences, those became my new direction. I didn't have the same interest in these fields as I once did for writing, but at least I had a way forward and I pushed onward.

This led to my work in conservation education for nonprofit organizations. Telling stories about wildlife and interacting with people filled me with joy. Yet, my long-term financial future looked bleak, and I felt the disorienting burden of needing to figure something else out.

When my parents suggested law school, I cringed at the idea. I knew nothing about law school. Yes, I had taken one class in environmental law during my undergraduate. But I never dreamed about or declared a desire to go to law school. When I browsed through the catalogue of law school courses, my eyes glazed over.

My parents reasoned that since I was good at writing and research, and I loved to speak on behalf of others, law school made logical sense. My chest contracted and I felt dread. Afraid of disappointing my parents and what I might lose if I didn't try, I ignored the messages of my body and applied for the LSAT.

I studied in secret. Aside from my family, no one else knew. When I received my test results, I had missed the passing score by a few points. I was relieved as I didn't want to go to law school, and yet I was dismayed by my failure. After all, I had recently graduated with a university gold medal for the highest academic standing in my faculty. With my chances for acceptance into law school low, I was still determined to prove my value; so I did my research and applied to the University of Ottawa.

Generally, law schools in Canada evaluate candidates based solely on their index score; this university took a broader approach. I pitched myself as a future environmental or animal law lawyer. When a large envelope arrived in the mail in the spring from the university, without opening it, I knew I had succeeded in pleading my case.

I was both satisfied and dismayed; my eyes brimmed with tears. I didn't know who I was or what I wanted, but this was definitely not it. But what else could a lost 22-year-old do with no other direction, guidance, or passion in sight?

Seeing the joy on my parents' faces further reinforced that I couldn't reject the offer. I publicly made an announcement to my friends a few weeks later about my acceptance. I was met with cheers of support, but I felt like an imposter for the first time in my life.

NEGLECTING THE MESSAGES of my body, I found myself wandering the halls of Fauteaux Hall. I felt uncomfortable in this new environment. Being among the many other law students who seemed smarter, more confident, and like they knew what they wanted and where they were going with their lives, left me thinking I was in the wrong place. Law school didn't help with its combination of Socratic teaching style, Latin jargon, and legal cases written in such a formal manner—it was like reading a novel from the 18th century again.

I was homesick, too. It was the first time I was living away from my family, friends, and the security I had always known. I felt confused and stressed a lot of the time. I didn't always comprehend what the law professors were saying to me, but I didn't dare express my insecurities to anyone. I couldn't be perceived as the weak one among all the shining stars.

I had a constant itching in my body to abandon my studies and return to Manitoba, Canada. Yet, I stayed because I had no idea what else I wanted to do. I was also terrified of my parents' reaction if I told them I was quitting law school. I pushed through the discomfort. By the end of the first year, I settled into a routine.

By the second year, I knew how to play the game. By the third year, I was getting bored and eager for it to end. My third year also brought me a deeper connection with the law school community. For most of the first two years, I avoided spending time with my peers outside of class. I didn't want my whole life to be about law school, so I built my community elsewhere. When I finally started spending time with my classmates, I discovered they were more like me than I had originally thought. They didn't have it all figured out either.

It was also toward the end of the second year that I gained insight into my interests. I arrived at law school with the belief that I would enjoy animal and environmental law – but I didn't. It was courses like restorative justice, family law, and interviewing and counselling that kindled my curiosity.

I regretted not exploring earlier what could be of interest to me, or taking the time to develop a stronger community in law school. Mostly, I had passively completed law school—like an act of defiance. Even though I didn't love environmental law, I kept taking related classes. I was apprehensive about the future and unable to lean into the possibilities of a different future as I had as a writer. By chance, I made some decisions that actually shifted my trajectory more in line with what I enjoyed.

By then, I had already secured my articling position at a nonprofit environmental law firm—a paid 10-month work experience that was mandatory to be eligible to be called to the bar in Canada. The position confirmed my lack of interest in environmental and animal law. I felt like I didn't know what I was doing, which made me feel anxious and tense in my body. Simultaneously, I was grateful for the 9 to 5 job I had landed and its kind lawyers. I had heard that other articling students were working 12-hour days to meet billable targets, and the lawyers they worked with weren't as nice. I knew I had it easy.

I SECURED MY FIRST official job as a lawyer within six months of my articling contract ending. I applied because it seemed like the next logical step in a legal career. I wanted a change so I accepted a position in northern Canada, in a small town of about 26,000 residents, a two-hour drive from the Alaska border. I arrived in January to freezing −40°F temperatures, a sun that rose after 10:00 am and set shortly after 3:00 pm and a mountainous landscape blanketed with snow. I started to wonder what I had gotten myself into.

I was sworn in as a lawyer before a Justice of the Supreme Court of Yukon soon after. Wearing white gloves to preserve the antiquity of the yellowing pages, I signed my name with a hopeful pride alongside all the other lawyers dating back over 100 years.

My new work was unrelated to environmental law, but it didn't take long before I was dissatisfied again. I spent most of the time alone in my office, staring at the computer screen for hours, conducting legal research, and writing memoranda for litigation files that seemed to have no end in sight. This was exacerbated by my growing anxiety, as thoughts of what I should've known by then coupled with thoughts that I really knew nothing intensified. Images of being "uncovered" for the fraud I was and being fired ran through my mind. My body tensed even more. I longed to work directly with people and to help clients more quickly.

Fortunately, there was a small aspect of my work that offered me the chance to work with clients. I became involved in a court-approved settlement process to the largest class action in Canadian history, worth over $3 billion. I acted as one of Canada's representatives in a unique alternative dispute resolution process compensating survivors of childhood sexual and physical abuses.[6] My main role was to listen to the oral testimony of claimants to determine the appropriate levels of abuse and resulting harms, and loss of income.

Despite the dark history and emotionally heavy nature of this work, I enjoyed it as it was in sharp contrast to all the other legal work I did. While there was some office work required to prepare for hearings, the most significant work took place in private law firm boardrooms or at a healing lodge. I interacted with and learned from other lawyers and adjudicators in a collaborative manner. Many of the files were resolved swiftly. There were always new issues arising that I didn't always know how to deal with, but I had so much support (especially from the Vancouver office) that I didn't feel alone or as anxious.

Within a year, I made the decision to leave that legal office, as I craved meaningful work for more than just part-time. When the opportunity arose to transfer to the Vancouver office to conduct settlement work full-time, it was another defining and empowering moment in my life. To transfer, I had to give up my full-time permanent government status. Many people consider this status a

---

[6] Over 150,000 indigenous children were forcefully removed from their homes across Canada for more than 100 years. They were placed into church-run, government-funded residential schools based on a policy of assimilation to "take the Indian out of the child." This cultural genocide continued until 1997 when the last school officially closed.

privilege and some even suggested I would be crazy to give it up. Yet, in my body, I experienced a whole-hearted, clear, expansive, joyful YES! I knew this was the right choice for me.

I felt right at home when I arrived at the Vancouver office. I was surrounded by an amazing team of more than 50 individuals committed to this work. I formed the closest friendships, had the most supportive manager—it was like being adopted into a big family and I couldn't have been happier.

AS PART OF FULL-TIME hearing work, I travelled regularly near and far, from British Columbia to Manitoba, up to the Arctic and even to the south near San Francisco. I commuted on ice roads, in small eight– to 20-seat passenger airplanes, on narrow rural high-ways, and busy multi-lane highways in big cities. Along the way, I grew an appreciation for the richness of Canada and developed fond memories on my work travels.

I drove through the dramatic volcanic landscape of the Nisga'a Memorial Lava Bed Park and the stunning peaks of the Rocky Mountains, in awe of their grandiose beauty. I strolled the beaches of Tofino, feeling the rhythmic flow of the Pacific Ocean on my bare feet. I browsed La Ronge's museum-like Robertson Trading Co., marveling at its walls decorated with taxidermied wildlife and indigenous art and culture. I climbed down a ladder into a dark underground freezer in Tuktoyaktuk, admiring the beautiful Arctic ice crystals in the spotlight of my flashlight.

I felt inspired by all the different worlds found in one country. My curiosity was aroused similar to the days when I would spend hours reading and writing. I started to make short videos of my adventures and shared them with family and colleagues who vicar-iously lived through me.

Travelling often meant I would work longer hours than usual. Sometimes I would be gone from my home from Sunday morning to Friday evening. Despite this, for the first year and a half, I was engulfed in deep happiness and gratitude. Anyone who showed any bitterness for their work, I couldn't understand. Anyone who left the workplace because they couldn't handle the stress, I considered them weak and foolish. Anyone who told me I would eventually stop enjoying travelling, I disbelieved.

FOR THE FIRST TIME in a long time, I felt alive again and the joy permeated throughout my entire body. To find such a perfect fit for myself in the legal field when I never thought I would was so meaningful.

Then it wasn't.

It wasn't truly sudden, but it seemed that way. I had been receiving many subtle messages from my body in the form of constricting sensations in my chest, thoughts that everything would be OK if I could just disconnect, and ongoing feelings of sadness and anxiety. These messages started in the first year of my work attending hearings part-time in the north. I noticed it especially after emotionally difficult files.

In many cases, the claimants I worked with were very still, quiet, and lacked emotion. They seemed frozen in time to when the events of their abuse had occurred in their childhood. It was through sharing their memories in their testimony that some of them would come to life with such an unexpected intensity that it almost always resulted in a complete emotional breakdown.

In the beginning, when I witnessed the child-like wailing of claimants, I found it both disturbing and baffling. I didn't understand why some of the claimants were having such explosive reactions often decades after the abuse happened. It was more perplexing—even irritating—when claimants who had experienced relatively low levels of abuse, compared to those with multiple and more serious abuses, continued to be such emotional wrecks. As I had been trained to be objective in law, I deemed emotions to be frivolous and distracting. They had no place at hearings for me—and neither did the messages from my body.

The truth is I was scared. I had finally found work that was fulfilling for me personally—while meaningful globally, as it contributed to healing and reconciliation. I feared losing my way again, of being directionless, having no purpose. I enjoyed my work with such eagerness; I didn't pay attention to any messages telling me a different story.

The compounding effect of being exposed to traumatic stories over five years built up an intensity of sensations, feelings, thoughts, and images I could no longer ignore. Just as the flame had flickered and then extinguished while I was struggling with writer's block, I could feel the same thing happening again.

In my trepidation, I focused my attention on controlling the environment to keep the joy alive and the internal intensity low. When the intensity started rising strongly a first and then a second time, I took two separate five-week holidays to visit my birth country of Poland and surrounding European cities. I had a merry time exploring new places with extended family.

I felt rejuvenated when I returned each time, but the feeling didn't last long. When I noticed the intensity arising strongly a third time, I took on an unrelated six-month office project to minimize the amount of travel and exposure. At the time, I had also started a part-time counselling training program. The first year was an exploration of self rather than professional skill development, and I needed to be local to attend classes.

A couple of months later, I agreed to attend a few hearings again. I noticed my hesitation immediately. Yet, I was restless from being in the office often. Plus, I reasoned the hearings were in a new geographic location so it would be good for me. Everything was fine until the hearing with the youngest claimant I had worked with to date—a 20-something. It wasn't a particularly emotional hearing, but it was a shock for me to work with a claimant who was in the thick of raging addictions and serious health problems. Due to the claimant's inability to offer testimony that day, the hearing had to be rescheduled.

The resistance in my body to attend a second time was strong. I didn't want to see this claimant again. I didn't want to be witness to the effects of this person's pain anymore. But I went anyway out of professional obligation and to avoid revealing my internal struggle to others.

I don't know why that claimant was such a trigger for me. Perhaps the person reflected my own increasingly numbed out state. Perhaps it was the counselling training program that was teaching me to be with, name, and express my emotions. Perhaps the harsh realities of the damage to indigenous people had become real for me.

Most of the claimants I had worked with were older. Many spoke of their past addictions and how it masked their pain. Many had overcome their addictions and were sober and in a better place at the time of their hearings. This claimant was in the midst of it all. This person was like the poster child of the horrors that had been imposed on indigenous people across Canada through abuse suffered at residential schools. It was all too real, too intense, too fast for me.

I began to destabilize at an expedited pace after this. I knew it was the work affecting me, but I still didn't understand why; nor was I ready to accept it. I resolved to find ways to control my environment so I could keep pushing through and doing this purposeful work.

I spent less time preparing for files and more time socializing with colleagues. During hearings, I didn't listen as intently or ask for as many details as I once had. But it wasn't enough. My ability to concentrate was already impaired. I became hypervigilant and hypersensitive. Even watching television was too intense for me—violence, anger, or swearing left my heart racing. I felt anxious, depressed, and paranoid. Then a seemingly innocuous event pushed me over the edge—a classmate from the counselling training program hugged me at a function. I had my first emotional breakdown in class while confronting the issue and interweaving the details with the suffering I had heard at hearings.

I must have been desperate because I ended up contacting the Lawyer's Assistance Program. But even when it was suggested that I go on sick leave because of likely vicarious trauma, I was mortified at the idea. I went back to work for one final week where I cried before hearings, triggering me into finally surrendering.

A psychologist diagnosed me with secondary traumatic stress and depression, and I took two months off. Convinced I was fine, I returned to the office. After only one day back and without even looking at my files once, I came home distressed and in tears. I took a leave of absence until my contract ended.

I had been fighting the messages of my body for so long and losing the battle every day. I felt the downpour of relief permeating throughout my body and I knew I had made the right choice again.

By chance, I found an amazing therapist. Building on the work I had done in the first year of the counselling training program, I learned even more about emotional regulation. To address my symptoms of post-traumatic stress, I engaged in Eye Movement Desensitization and Reprocessing. I felt worse after some sessions and better after others. After nearly a year, I stopped going to therapy. I felt better overall, but the familiar thought of having lost my way reappeared and I desired to find my way.

I DIDN'T WANT TO WORK in a legal capacity or to become a counsellor anymore, as I worried something would go wrong again. I also couldn't imagine finding as meaningful of a legal position again. So I explored different avenues. I spent a summer gold-mining near historic Dawson City. I dabbled in freelance writing for travel magazines. I went back to Europe to explore new cities. I participated in transformational group coaching and leadership programs. I practiced yoga, meditation, and breathwork. I even co-founded a construction company a few years later.

This was a period of growth for me. But I continually noticed something felt off in my body. It was like a low-grade anxiety mixed with a hopeless helplessness that I couldn't shake off no matter what I did.

Then the pandemic struck and I started taking part in online embodiment circles. They were an opportunity for intentional connection and movement; I loved how energized I felt afterward. This led me to the work of Dr. Stephen Porges' Polyvagal theory and then Steven Hoskinson's Organic Intelligence®. Neither body of work was easy to understand as they were both based on the functioning of the nervous system—they were complex and riddled in esoteric language and this often frustrated me. Yet, a spacious inquisitiveness kept insisting this was something I wanted to know. I followed my impulse and devoured as many resources as I could find with the enthusiasm of my youth.

Powerful insights about the body, the nervous system, and trauma were slowly unveiled to me. Although I had worked with trauma survivors for five years, it was only after exposure to these theories that I finally understood the disorganizing effect of trauma and stress on the body. The behavior of the claimants and my own experiences with secondary traumatic stress, combined with the inability to truly feel better and the "yoyoing" between feeling lost and scared to grasping for direction and purpose throughout my life, suddenly made sense to me.

I learned that all behavior reflects the state of a person's nervous system. This shepherded my breakthrough in healing. Counterintuitive to what I had experienced in previous attempts to feel better, the pathway to healing wasn't about suffering through painful sensations, feelings, thoughts, and images. Rather, the pathway to healing was through community connection, embodied pleasure, and authentic humanity.

As I began to engage in simple daily practices, the state of my nervous system gently produced stability. I learned to be with and understand the subtle messages of my body, ending my era of disembodied living. I experienced more curiosity, equanimity, and creativity. When stressful or other challenging moments elevated my internal intensity, I learned how to lower it in a natural and pleasurable way. In the process, I grew my capacity to handle more complexity. I became more present, mindful, and open to the possibilities. I reveled in stillness, and my trust and belief in "self" returned with a level of vehemence like never before.

THE FLAME FROM WITHIN shone brightly again and with a maturity and wisdom evolved from my younger years of writing fiction with fervor. I realized it had always been there, it had simply dimmed over the disorganizing years of my own stresses and the exposure to other people's trauma. With a newfound aliveness and inspiration, I am now immersed in the study of embodiment, what it means to be truly human and the functioning of the nervous system—especially through the work of Organic Intelligence®. It was the missing piece on my healing journey, and it could be the missing piece on your journey, too.

My inability to be with the messages of my body is how I ended up being a lawyer.

Even though it wasn't what I wanted, the experience guided me on a fruitful adventure of discovering and befriending the hidden obvious—the human being with its body and nervous system in all its supportive magnificence.

CHAPTER FOURTEEN

Balancing the Fundamentals

by Elena Kohn

"My definition of success can be succinctly captured in these numbers: being married to my best friend for 20 years this fall, raising 2 beautiful children, and practicing law for 10 years in an area that is constantly developing. "

I WAS 10 YEARS OLD when the Soviet Union collapsed. The world as I knew it turned upside down. Instability and chaos ensued. Prices for the most basic of items, such as food, skyrocketed overnight. Food supply became scarce.

Prior to that, both my parents had been professionals with a stable income employed in a state-funded system, virtually unchanged for decades. When the system collapsed, so did their income. There were three of us young siblings. Suddenly, our parents were unable to feed us.

Can you imagine?

To provide for us, they had to swallow their pride and improvise, hauling their possessions to an outdoor winter market to sell what they could.

Extreme hardship continued for a number of years.

That brutal period following the collapse of the Soviet Union, with its lawlessness, corruption, and societal disintegration, took a toll on all of us. Still a child, I watched as my parents were consumed by stress. I saw my mother's health deteriorate. Our local hospital, rendered dysfunctional by chronic corruption, lacked the basic equipment to detect her cancer when it still might have been possible to save her.

When she confronted them later, indifferent hospital administrators merely shrugged and said, "Go ahead and sue us."

There was no recourse, no accountability—and everyone knew it.

It was this experience that first ignited my passion for the law. I dreamed of living in a more stable, law-based society, where individual rights could be protected.

Some years passed, one thing led to another, and my husband and I found ourselves leaving Russia for the United Kingdom (U.K.). There, I graduated college and enrolled in the College of Law to pursue my dream of becoming a lawyer.

It was also there that my son was born and my life was changed forever. Being a mother meant a new, higher purpose—caring for someone vulnerable and being responsible for everything that happened to that young life.

AFTER SEVEN YEARS in the U.K., we moved to the United States in 2007 and I applied to law school. Never had I imagined that I would be accepted right away, especially because I knew several people with similar backgrounds whose applications had been rejected. Receiving an acceptance letter was one of the most joy-filled days of my life, perhaps only similar to my wedding day and the day my son was born.

When I went to law school, my son was 4 years old. My story is proof that motherhood and career aspirations are not mutually exclusive. On the contrary, motherhood gives a lawyer superpowers.

It is because I had a little one waiting for me at home while I was in law school that I made every minute and every second spent studying count, since it was time spent away from my son. I did not party and I did not waste a moment of precious time. Instead, I worked hard and graduated near the top of my class, all while being the only immigrant in my class for whom English was not my native language.

I was laser focused on my studies and career because, once again, that was time taken away from my son.

Being a non-native speaker, I had to work extra hard in law school. Once, in Corporations class, we were analyzing a case that had been assigned for home reading, and the word "eleemosynary" came up. The professor asked if anyone knew what it meant. None of the other students did (there were about 60 of us), so I raised my hand.

You see, because English is not my native language, I would routinely spend extra hours reading the assigned case law and looking up the meaning of every single word I was unsure about.

Was it laborious? You bet! But that's what it took to overcome my language deficit—a necessary step on my long journey to success. And in the process, I also picked up some "twenty-dollar" words that nobody uses, such as "eleemosynary." You've got to look that one up!

I AM GRATEFUL THAT law school gave me an opportunity to intern for a couple of federal judges. Most impressive to me was a federal judge in the Middle District of Florida. She had been the only woman in her law school graduating class. She rose to the top of her profession and was an inspirational jurist. Watching her in open court was a thing of beauty. Her fast wit and dauntless demeanor, coupled with compassion, will remain with me forever.

When I graduated law school, 52% of our graduating class were women. Top grades were often earned by women. Yet, when I started practicing, I saw very few women occupying the top positions in their law firms.

This felt strange.

Up to that point, my personal experience led me to believe in equal opportunities in the legal industry. Unfortunately, the industry was severely lagging behind in recognizing women's potential in critical areas, such as work ethic, perseverance, teamwork mentality, tenaciousness, desire to mentor, and natural business development skills.

When in law school, I was interviewed by several law firms. One of them no longer exists. That particular firm's recruitment practices left me speechless. During my interview, the senior associate asked me the following questions, in rapid succession:

(1) Are you married?

(2) Do you have children?

(3) Do you have tattoos anywhere on your body?

Note, this was not too long ago, still in the 21st century. Fortunately for me, I ended up working in a much more professional environment.

IN THE LEGAL INDUSTRY in the United States, it is considered prestigious and highly coveted to secure a place in a BigLaw firm after graduation. Through hard work, lots of determination, good grades, and interpersonal skills, I was able to secure such a spot.

BigLaw attorneys have notoriously high annual billable-hour requirements. Yet, not every minute of an attorney's time is billable. Generally, administrative tasks are not billable. In order for a young associate (also known as a "baby lawyer" in the industry) to bill eight hours a day, that associate likely needs to spend 10–11 hours in the office. Long hours and weekend work are typical.

This is why the industry is experiencing burnout.

It's a lack of balance.

BigLaw jobs are prestigious and the perks are great; but it is not everyone's definition of success.

I worked in BigLaw for a couple of years; during that time, I missed a number of my son's baseball games and other important events. During a pivotal moment, I distinctly remember being in my office for the 12th or 13th hour that day, when I looked around.

I noticed senior partners sitting in their gorgeous offices equipped with the latest tech, with beautiful views of downtown (honestly, though, nobody ever had time to look outside because of the billable hours).

Senior partners had assigned parking spots in the parking garage and they drove the latest model Porsche. These partners were high earners and were considered by all standards a total success. Yet, their marriages were crumbling and they were not on speaking terms with their children.

That moment was a defining one for me.

It was that "Eureka" moment when I realized that while I admired these people's incredible focus and niche expertise in their respective areas—developed over decades—it was not my definition of success. It seemed too imbalanced, lacking in something I considered fundamental.

My definition of success can be succinctly captured in these numbers: being married to my best friend for 20 years this fall, raising 2 beautiful children, and practicing law for 10 years in an area that is constantly developing.

This success entails working very hard, yet it emphasizes balance and being a whole person. Being involved in my children's lives makes me a more compassionate person, which, in turn, makes me a better counselor to my corporate client.

You see, attorneys are not simply machines who can conduct legal research and regurgitate rules of law. We are advisors and counselors to our clients; those roles require us to possess a high Emotional Quotient. Honestly, who better than a mother to relate to a personal struggle and use that understanding to advise more compassionately on an issue of law?

The realization that my definition of success was antithetical to a BigLaw lifestyle resulted in my obtaining an in-house job with one of the firm's clients. The client, who was in healthcare, was happy with my work and decided that it would be more cost-efficient to employ me directly.

I have been practicing as an in-house attorney in the healthcare space ever since.

DURING MY TIME AS an in-house attorney, our family grew, and we added a spunky little girl who for the longest time believed she was the last-living Tyrannosaurus Rex. My daughter knows that women can become anything they want: a CEO, a doctor, a lawyer, an astronaut, an explorer, a homemaker—anything at all (maybe not a T-Rex). Representation and role models matter; and my daughter gets to observe me every day working hard for my client and my family, as I am now a Vice President of the company.

Were sacrifices made along the way? Absolutely. I had to return to work after maternity leave when my daughter was only 9 weeks old. There is a picture of her somewhere as a little baby sitting in my huge office chair on a brief lunchtime visit after I had just returned to work. Leaving her and returning to work when she was so young was very hard, but it was the right decision for my family.

Like many professional women, I made the decision to continue breastfeeding my daughter even after returning to work full time, due to the tremendous benefits of breast milk for infants as documented by numerous scientific studies.

Workplaces tend not to be designed with breastfeeding mothers in mind.

I remember in one of my prior jobs, portraits of male aristocrats decorated the walls of the lactation room. These men had a sort of Mona Lisa stare that followed you to every corner of the lactation room.

It felt uncomfortable.

I believe that having to navigate through uncomfortable personal circumstances definitely makes you a better advocate and a better lawyer. When I started my first General Counsel job, I remember locking the door for a brief spell to use the pump; my then CEO knocked on the door to remind me that we had an open door policy at the company.

I remember explaining to him that I did not think my colleagues would have appreciated the view of me pumping milk for my newborn.

He turned red and never mentioned it again.

What does my current job entail? I help a national ObGyn group with its legal work. This involves reviewing healthcare regulations, employment law items, employment agreements, corporation resolutions, commercial leases, large contracts within the context of the highly regulated healthcare space, and anything else you can imagine in-house counsel for a large company would deal with.

Advising clients and guiding them through difficult situations are part-and-parcel of the job. I report to the group's General Counsel, who is an inspiring and strong woman, prioritizing her team's balance to ensure burnout is avoided. This ensures continuity of the team and produces long-term success for the client.

THROUGHOUT, I CANNOT emphasize enough the unconditional support of my husband. He stood by me through thick and thin, through successes and failures, through law school and the challenges that followed when I first became a lawyer.

My husband has significantly contributed to the development of our children. To him, equal co-parenting is not just a fad or some unrealistic request. Children benefit from having both parents present and impactful in their lives. This calls for more balanced legal jobs for both men and women.

As my professional life continues to develop, I sometimes pause to think how fortunate I have been throughout the years to have a strong support system at home. This has led to incredible career opportunities.

If you are reading this chapter, and if I can ever be of service in talking to you about your career journey, please do not hesitate to reach me on LinkedIn.

CHAPTER FIFTEEN

Making an Impact

by Maja Larson

> *"I have friends who are like siblings, providing me love and support when I need it. I have had professional mentors throughout my career who have pushed me to do more than what I thought was possible, convincing me that I was capable of so much more."*

ACCORDING TO DICTIONARY.COM, "success" means "the favorable or prosperous termination of attempts or endeavors; the accomplishments of one's goals," and "the attainment of wealth, position, honors, or the like."

If one looks at my LinkedIn profile or my CV, I have reached "success" in my career. I graduated with honors from the University of Washington's Sociology program and *magna cum laude* from Seattle University School of Law. I worked at one of the largest law firms in Seattle, and as a first-year associate, I served on the team that handled the Expedia IPO; then I worked for Expedia for several years.

I served as General Counsel to the Allen Institute, an independent nonprofit medical research organization founded by the late

Paul G. Allen. I was nominated twice for Corporate Counsel of the Year in the *Puget Sound Business Journal*. I published a book chapter with a professor at Seattle University Law. I have been an adjunct professor at Seattle University Law for the past eight years and consistently receive positive reviews from my class, including "best class I took in law school."

However, none of that "success" makes me feel successful. That "success" is the culmination of what I am paid to do. It is not what makes me the successful woman I am. To me, I am successful because I have been intentional with making an impact and overcoming challenges throughout my career.

TO REACH ANY LEVEL of success in my life, no matter the definition, I had to overcome challenges. I am the product of a middle-class, single-parent household. My mother worked hard to take care of her children, all of whom had emotional and mental health issues except for me. I was the only child who finished high school, let alone college and graduate school.

When I graduated high school, I received college scholarships for academic performance; unfortunately, I had no idea what to do with them because I had no college counseling and no one to explain how to apply for college. At the time, I suffered from other obstacles—I lacked confidence, I was painfully shy, and I constantly felt like an imposter because I did not belong with any group. Yet, at no point did these obstacles deter me from becoming successful. I am successful not because of these obstacles but in spite of these obstacles.

I could go through my career and all the challenges I have overcome, but instead I will share how I intentionally overcame those challenges. My career serves as a winding and diverse pathway of examples of how I have overcome many hurdles and achieved success—while learning a few lessons along the way:

❖ Without a strong family to teach me the basics, I chose friends' family members, teachers, and other mentors and supporters to teach me things that I did not understand, and I learned that continuing to build this network is important. I have friends who are like siblings, providing me love and support when I need it. I have had professional mentors throughout my career who have pushed me to do more than what I thought was possible, convincing me that I was capable of so much more. I surround myself with supporters who help with my imposter and confidence issues.

❖ These people are part of the fabric of my success to which I owe so much gratitude. For example, a man I dated, who was 15 years my senior, helped me apply to the University of Washington when I was 24. He did this knowing that once I was accepted, we would probably break up because I would be around people my own age (and we did).

❖ I put myself in uncomfortable situations. I am reminded of a quote from Greek philosopher Epictetus who wrote in Enchiridion 33.14:

"In public, avoid talking often and excessively about your accomplishments and dangers, for how much you enjoy recounting your dangers, it's not so pleasant for others to hear about your affairs."

I am shy and humble and the limelight makes me very uncomfortable. However, I knew I needed to get out in front if I was going to ever be successful in my career. Over the years, I have accepted many opportunities to speak on panels. In addition, I make a point of attending networking events and I teach at a law school. These are not comfortable for me to do, even after many years of doing them. But I do it because after each encounter, I feel more confident and more successful, even if the encounter was not exactly the way I wanted it to be. I have learned to not hold myself to a perfect standard or to compare myself to others in the same situation. Our interactions are all unique and my folksy style is what makes me unique.

- ❖ I use alternative therapies and coaching to break through barriers. I have consistently sought out ways to break through mental and emotional barriers to stay balanced in my life. While talk therapy is great for many people, it is not effective for me because it does not let me reflect inward enough. I have successfully used a method called voice dialogue, which focuses on developing self-awareness. More recently, I have participated in coaching and practicing the principles of positive intelligence (from the book *Positive Intelligence* by Shirzad Chamine) to understand barriers and continue growth. Whatever the method, I believe everyone can benefit from finding ways to effectively understand more about themselves.

- ❖ I do not try to fit in as one of the men. As much as I do not want to admit it, I believe that my being a woman served as an obstacle in my professional life. For most of my career, I have been the single female in a room full of men. I never expect to be treated any differently; I do, however, expect to be treated equally. I choose not to be forceful about it; in fact, I would rather it be genuine and organic. It does not always pan out the way I want it to, but I have learned to hold my ground. I was told I was not leadership material at one point; but rather than push back, I bided my time and waited patiently for the perfect opportunity to make my move.

THROUGHOUT MY OVER 30-year career, I have worked outside of my job description to do more than was required, but not for the career growth or kudos. I am driven to make more impact—to make things more efficient, mentor more people, support more of the business to help it grow.

During my tenure at the Allen Institute, I was not feeling impactful enough personally and chose to start teaching law at Seattle University to educate and mentor law students. Fast forward to 2021, at the age of 56, I left what is probably my last in-house counsel position. It was fulfilling to work for a nonprofit organization for 14 years and that was impactful, but my position was no longer fulfilling for me. I want to be more impactful—in more diverse ways—and I am confident that I will be successful with whatever path I choose to follow moving forward.

Why am I so confident?

- ❖ I am naturally focused on making an impact.

- ❖ I like to think and work outside the box, which is more interesting and fulfilling, and allows me to be more innovative and impactful.

- ❖ I see the glass as more than half full—to find the best in and to learn the most from every experience.

- ❖ I am not afraid to take advantage of an opportunity, and to make the most of it, without second-guessing my decision.

- ❖ I ask questions, am intellectually curious, and have a strong desire to learn deeply about many things. I am not afraid of saying I do not know the answer, or I need more information.

❖ I do not feel successful unless those around me are equally successful; I strongly believe that it takes a village, and every person is an important part of the village.

The world changed during the pandemic. There has always been business networking; but now there is a need for real camaraderie, as we have spent the last two years finding ways to connect on Zoom. We all seem to be aiming for a similar North Star of true personal fulfillment in our careers and lives, and finding that it is not only possible but required.

I used to be a quiet internal force, overcoming obstacles and being intentional with my desire to make an impact. But the pandemic changed all of that. I quit my job and became part of the "Great Resignation," thinking I would not work in a 9-to-5 job again.

Since separating from the Allen Institute, I have focused on paying it forward for all the love and support that I received during my career. I now share candidly and listen intently to connect in a way that I have not done before. I am not working in a traditional legal career, but I am using my experience, knowledge, skills, and expertise in many capacities—as an adjunct law professor, advisory board member, investor, board member, mentor, connector, and friend.

It is empowering, motivating, and impactful; and that makes me very successful ... in my book.

CHAPTER SIXTEEN

Striking a Balance

by Nhu-Y Le

> *"Success for me is setting a good example for my team on how to balance life and work and to showcase that worthiness comes from within. I still fail to do this on some days, but I am a work in progress."*

"WELL, ISN'T THIS AWKWARD?"

I stood outside my manager's office, waiting for her to wrap up a meeting so that I could inform her of my big announcement. Every few seconds, I nervously looked down at my phone's home screen at a picture. My husband and I had dressed as Ash and Pikachu for Halloween. We're both looking directly at the camera, and we're sitting close to each other with big, toothy smiles. At that moment, I realized just how much I missed him.

We had met on an online dating site in 2011, shortly after I moved to Boston for law school. He had recently moved back to Boston for graduate school. Our first date was in Harvard Square, where we got to know each other over beers in a basement bar and cheap pizza by the slice. Fast forward through several years of dating, law school, the stress of the bar exam, and a short stint apart when I moved to Northern Virginia for my first job after graduation, we finally tied the knot in 2015.

Life stabilized after we married and we were excited to build a shared life together. I'd found work at a large business immigration law firm in the heart of Boston. My husband continued chipping away at his PhD dissertation in Theoretical Physics. We rented an apartment in a cute neighborhood within walking distance to hipster coffee shops and great restaurants. We were the typical mid-twenties, educated, cosmopolitan, and child-free couple.

We should have been happy with our newlywed life. We were young and in love. We would have been happy, except that I was mentally and physically depleted by the time I arrived home from work every night. I had zero time or energy to spend with my husband. During the busy season at work, it was common for me to eat dinner at the law firm and work until 10:30 pm, and then take an Uber home. I would wake up at 6:00 am every morning to answer work emails, then take the train to work at 8:30 am.

Work. Dinner at work. Uber home. Rinse and repeat.

Even though I loved the work, the demanding schedule and caseload were draining. I was constantly exhausted, short-tempered, and moody. I was quickly burning out.

WHEN A RECRUITER reached out via LinkedIn about an in-house counsel opportunity at a large software company, I felt like the "career gods" had thrown me a lifeline. I thought that going in-house would solve everything. After all, I had heard so many glowing stories of attorneys transitioning to in-house roles and finally achieving a healthy work-life balance for the first time in their careers. I enthusiastically accepted the interview request.

When the recruiter called back weeks later to announce that I had been offered the position, I was ecstatic and couldn't wait to share the news with my husband. I fantasized about the new job and all the potential it held.

The only catch was that this job was on the other side of the country. We were living in our cozy apartment outside of Boston and the job offer was for Seattle—with no possibility for remote work.

Initially, when I accepted the interview, I knew that the position was in Seattle. I'd gone ahead with the interview because I wanted to challenge myself to explore career options outside of the traditional law firm setting. It felt good to be considered for an in-house counsel position at a Fortune 100 company. I was still relatively junior in my career and didn't think I was going to get the job. Now that the job offer was miraculously in my hand, this was no longer just a fanciful dream. My husband and I needed to make a life-changing decision about our future.

On one hand, I desperately wanted to give Seattle a try. A job that I didn't think I could get was officially mine for the taking. I felt that this was my dream job. This was the job that would make everything better for us. On the other hand, my husband was wrapping up his PhD dissertation and an internship with the federal government in Boston. He couldn't move across the country right away.

After several weighty conversations, we ultimately decided that I would relocate to Seattle alone at first, to settle into the new role and test out whether Seattle was truly a good fit for our new home. In the meantime, my husband would remain in Boston to finish his degree. We had successfully done long-distance dating before and felt confident that we had the trust and communication skills required to try a long-distance marriage.

I landed in Seattle in late November 2016, buzzing with excitement. I was in a new part of the country by myself. Everything was new and fresh, and I loved everything I saw. The company had arranged for me to stay in corporate housing while I searched for an apartment. I was in awe.

The evergreens were so lush. Mt. Rainer was so majestic. My new coworkers were friendly and intelligent. The campus cafeterias had an array of delicious lunch options from different cuisines around the world. There was even free coconut water and fruit-infused water throughout the office buildings. My heart leapt with joy because I felt I had made the right decision to join the in-house legal team.

My husband and I video chatted every night, and I eagerly shared my new adventures in Seattle with him. We settled into a comfortable routine of catching up after dinner. A temporary, long-distance marriage seemed doable, and we were proud of ourselves for making the space for each other to achieve our career goals.

THEN, LIFE HAPPENED.

My period was late in December 2016. I chalked this up to the stress of moving across the country and starting a new job. I brushed it off because I wanted to dive into my new role and socialize with my new coworkers in my new city.

Three days later, still no period.

One week later, still no period.

When the weekend arrived, I finally decided to buy an at-home pregnancy test. It was highly unusual for my period to be this late. Could I be pregnant?

I peed on the test strip and waited. Within two minutes, two distinct pink lines emerged. The instructions pamphlet delineated that two lines meant PREGNANT. I stared at the test strip in shock, slowly processing the new information.

I took a second test to be sure. Two lines again. Definitely pregnant.

I hurriedly video-called my husband and showed him the test results, partly because I wanted to share the news with my partner and because I was still in disbelief. His face lit up with joy. We were going to be parents! Sure, the timing wasn't ideal. I had just moved to Seattle a little over a month ago and we were temporarily living across the country from each other; but we could make this work. We were going to be a family of three soon!

We contemplated when to share the good news with family, friends, and my company. In particular, I had reservations about when to share the pregnancy with my new manager. I'd just started this dream job several weeks earlier and had not yet formed a strong rapport with my manager. How was she going to react to this news? Should I wait to tell her? Should I let her know right away?

Ultimately, I decided to share the news immediately with my manager because I calculated that providing transparency and giving her as much notice as possible was the best I could do in this situation.

I LOOKED UP FROM my phone when I saw my manager's office door open and a coworker walking out. It was my turn. My manager motioned for me to come in.

We made small talk to ease into the conversation. I was so distracted with anticipation of the pregnancy announcement that I can't even remember what we chatted about. It may have been how no one uses umbrellas in Seattle, our weekend plans, or the new snacks we bought from Costco. The topics blended together.

When I gauged that an acceptable level of small talk had been achieved, I blurted out, "I don't know how to tell you this. This is not good timing, but I'm pregnant."

There's no manual or best practice on how to tell your manager at your dream job that you just started that you are pregnant. I admit the way I shared the news was not the most graceful.

I braced myself for impact.

To my surprise, the news landed smoothly. My manager congratulated me and thanked me for letting her know. She, too, was a mother and kindly shared her experience with pregnancy, childbirth, and motherhood. I left the meeting feeling supported and hopeful for my future as a working mom.

AS THE WEEKS PROGRESSED, the pregnancy turned out to be much more difficult than I had anticipated. I did not have the pregnancy glow. In fact, I was ashen, sick, and queasy most of the time.

I was diagnosed with Hyperemesis Gravidarum, which is a severe form of morning sickness characterized by frequent nausea and vomiting throughout the pregnancy. I would nibble on crystallized ginger on my morning bus ride to work in an attempt to mitigate the wave of nausea. This barely helped.

I threw up all the time. It was a regular occurrence for me to throw up near the bus stop because I could not make it to a bathroom in time. I threw up in the trash can in my office several times a week—sometimes before and after a client call. I threw up in the sink in the break room. Eventually, I needed to be medicated for the severe vomiting and nausea.

At the 24-week checkup, I was also diagnosed with gestational diabetes. I had to administer a hand prick blood test several times a day to monitor my blood sugar levels. Seeing blood when you are constantly nauseous and dry heaving is a below-optimal combination.

Through all of this, I continued to work. The Trump administration had rolled out a Muslim travel ban in early 2017, which was the first of a series of executive orders restricting entry into the United States for citizens of mostly Muslim countries. These immigration changes wreaked havoc for our visa-dependent employees. We had employees stranded abroad, and people had to arrange last-minute flights to enter the United States before the executive order took effect. The entire immigration team at the company worked overtime to serve as a pillar of legal and emotional support for employees through these dramatic changes.

I pushed myself to work more and to work harder. I worked late into the night to answer emails from panicked employees. Looking back, I probably pushed myself too hard. Pregnant women with gestational diabetics need to eat regular, high protein and low carb meals to control their blood sugar. I am ashamed to admit that I would sometimes become so wrapped up with work that I would skip lunch or dinner. I wasn't getting the nutrition or the rest my growing baby needed.

I had heaped enormous pressure on myself to demonstrate my worth to the company. I was competing with myself. I'd set a high standard to outperform and work hard because I wanted to prove to the company that it had made the right decision to hire me. I felt that I had something to prove as a pregnant employee. Even though the company and my manager were supportive of my pregnancy, I was my personal drill sergeant. Obviously, this was not a healthy mindset for an expectant mother with two pregnancy-related medical conditions.

About halfway through my pregnancy, everything felt bleak. I was not taking care of myself mentally or physically. It was a real-life reenactment of a scene from a generic Hallmark movie. I was slumped on the kitchen floor, my back to the dishwasher, sobbing because I was so stressed with work. I was feeling so alone in Seattle. I was worried about the impact my mental state of mind was having on the baby.

My husband lovingly talked me through some of the darkest moments during my pregnancy. We made plans to expedite his move to Seattle because I was spiraling out of control on my own.

Through all of this, miraculously, no one at work knew the extent of the turmoil in my personal life. I tried to maintain a professional presence at work. I tried to be upbeat and cheerful. Instead of scaling back, I took on more work. I didn't ask for the help I needed from coworkers or my manager because I was in a dangerous competition with myself to show that I belonged.

MY HUSBAND EXPEDITED his PhD defense and singlehandedly wrapped up our affairs in Boston as quickly as he could. He joined me in Seattle in June 2017, and his physical presence helped to balance out my nerves.

When I am alone, my natural inclination is to overwork. My definition of success was how hard I could push myself to work to generate outcomes and prove my value. The factors for success were rigid, internally hypercompetitive, and dangerously unhealthy. I was constantly putting my mental and physical well-being in jeopardy.

My husband kept the guardrails on for the remainder of my pregnancy. He made sure that I ate, drank enough water, took walks, and got enough rest each day.

We welcomed our healthy baby boy into the world on September 6, 2017. In our eyes, our baby was perfect in every way. Although the pregnancy was harrowing, he was worth it. I nuzzled my nose against his soft cheeks in the maternity ward, and made a pledge that I was going to be the best mom I could be to this small human who now completely depended on us.

WHERE AM I NOW? Did everything work out? Was the birth of my son the miracle solution for my unhealthy work-life balance and desire to prove myself at work?

No, of course, not.

I love my son unconditionally. I tell him he is my "sun, and star, and Milky Way." But no single person can change anyone else; I am a firm believer that change has to come from within.

I know that I have an unhealthy relationship with work. I define success by my work. I derive immense personal satisfaction from pleasing others at work. I have an insatiable need to prove to others that I can do the job well and that I belong.

What I've learned is that moving across the country for a dream job, changing from a law firm to an in-house role, and having a child were not going to change my toxic relationship with work. I needed to create a healthier mindset.

I'm trying to change. I've been working one-on-one with a career coach on techniques to lower my susceptibility to burnout. I am learning to delegate, ask for help, trust my team, and grow my emotional intelligence so that I am not in a losing competition with myself on my worthiness for a role. I aim to define success as finding balance and being kind to myself.

I am currently leading a large team at Legalpad, an innovative immigration legal tech startup, and other female lawyers report to me. To normalize motherhood and leadership, I make it a point to talk about my son frequently at work and post pictures of him on the company's internal social channels. Being pregnant or being a mother should not mean that you must work harder to demonstrate your value as an employee.

Success for me is setting a good example for my team on how to balance life and work and to showcase that worthiness comes from within.

I still fail to do this on some days, but I am a work in progress.

CHAPTER SEVENTEEN

No Superpowers Needed

by Krista Lynn

"Today, I am 'just' a Superwoman in recovery; a woman who has come to the realization that I do not have to do everything for anyone, let alone everyone, particularly at the sacrifice of my own hopes, dreams, and plans."

MY NAME IS KRISTA LYNN, and I am a Recovering Superwoman. Technically, I'm THE Recovering Superwoman; that is, if social media presence transcends real life.

I am so tempted to begin my story by telling you about the hats I wear.

All the hats.

Especially the UCF baseball cap (Go, Knights!) that I proudly wear during college football season (and anytime I don't want to do my hair). Definitely the purple fascinator that I got when attending a bourgeois horse race in Galway, Ireland, during a summer study abroad. And I simply cannot skip the tan Panama hat that I like to wear with a cute sundress all summer long.

Wait, did I say hats? I mean my other hats—the proverbial ones.

The hats that I wear in my life, namely, the roles that I play and the things I do that make me who I am:

- ❖ I am endlessly optimistic.

- ❖ Passion runs through my veins.

- ❖ I need challenges in my life like I need air.

- ❖ I am occasionally lazy.

- ❖ I live to celebrate moments, big and small—preferably with champagne.

- ❖ I crave deep conversation and respectful debate of any kind.

- ❖ Celine Dion is literally the tops for me; my obsession is real.

- ❖ Sometimes I overcommit.

- ❖ I get frustrated with silence.

- ❖ I am a hopeless romantic.

- ❖ I put other people ahead of myself, too often.

- ❖ I inhale joy when I'm with my kids.

- ❖ Effort is sexy.

- ❖ I am tired more than I wish to admit.

- ❖ I am codependent.

- ❖ I don't think I'm pretty.

- ❖ I miss practicing martial arts.

- ❖ I am stubborn.

- ❖ I love feeling like I'm in control, but also love losing it.

- ❖ I make mistakes.

❖ I pray hard. Sometimes I worry harder.

But, wait, if I list all those hats, then the "recovering" part of my self-imposed Recovering Superwoman title wouldn't be very accurate. While recovery for me is a never-ending quest to reach the North Star, I'd like to think there's some truth to the title. And to become a Recovering Superwoman, I needed to focus a lot less on "what I do" and more on "who I am" and "what matters to me."

FOR MOST OF MY life, I have had an achievement addiction. I used to consider the desire for high achievement to be a positive thing. It can be. After all, self-motivation is usually a highly sought-after character trait for potential employees. But somewhere in my childhood, I learned that I could earn love, attention, and affection by getting good grades, excelling in my extracurricular activities, and otherwise doing exactly what I was told.

Healthy achievement can and should be rewarding. Fulfilling, even. The problem comes when your sense of self becomes attached to your ability to achieve.

One of the biggest negatives in the pursuit of achievement is that it takes away from the deeply ordinary things that make life meaningful. Being Superwoman becomes the goal, as if "woman" in 2022 isn't an achievement enough these days (I'm looking at you, Texas).

For me, the addiction to being extraordinary didn't magically disappear with coming of age or even adulthood. Rather, it magnified. The external validation that came with doing things that were beyond what people expected of me, personally and professionally, was thrilling. Whether it was getting a deal done that was labeled "impossible"; working with colleagues who were deemed "difficult";

or solving a problem that no one else could figure out, I ate up the praise and admiration that would come my way.

The addiction to success was more important to me than being happy. In fact, I completely lost track of who and what even made me happy. And that's part of the reason I found myself in an abusive relationship.

Don't be fooled, though. You probably wouldn't have known it unless you were my next-door neighbor and witnessed the police cars being regularly dispatched to my house. For the most part, I carefully curated a life in pictures and statements that made it seem like I had it all—because, of course, Superwoman has to have it all; it's part of what makes her a Superwoman. I had the "perfect" house that was always clean, the "perfect" career progression, and the "perfect" family.

SO MUCH FOR BEING honest with myself; at least now, I can be honest with you.

I was dealing with a spouse in active addiction and the mental health issues that usually accompany such a plight. My life was a mess because someone intimately close to me was wreaking havoc on it faster than I could clean up the damage. And since we're being honest, I have to tell you: I am pretty sure I knew it at the time that the image I portrayed was not complete or remotely accurate. I have never been naïve or accused of lacking self-awareness. I was just too deep in the fog to do anything else.

Even now with the benefit of seven years of regular counseling and therapy, I still occasionally experience bouts of haziness regarding parts of my life from that period. Every so often, something seemingly random—a commercial, a fleeting thought in the middle of the night, or a question by a stranger—will trigger a repressed memory. My abuse recovery coach tells me that moments like those can be expected as my emotions finally start to feel safe to surface after years of living in "fight or flight" mode—a situation where there is no room for emotion.

Destruction was aplenty in my home life, and I truly do not know how I was able to stay employed, keep my kids healthy and safe, and not lose my mind. I can only surmise that doing so contributed to my idea of being Superwoman, especially because no one really knew what life was really like behind the scenes.

I remember thinking, "If they only knew what I was dealing with at the same time I closed that deal, then they'd really think I was something!" There was a little bit of a high that I got from knowing I could kick ass and take names while simultaneously managing some of what I considered to be the darkest days of my life.

I THOUGHT I HAD TO "achieve" in my marriage—which, in hindsight, merely surviving it should be considered an accomplishment. Achieving was all I had going for me. During a lifetime of chasing that next success, unfortunately, I failed to develop a sense of "self" underneath it all. My now ex-husband had to get his sh*t together, or I would see it as a failure on my part. I was going to will it to be, even if and especially if he couldn't—because I was Superwoman.

But you cannot make people act in a way that is contrary to their internal motivations, at least not for the long haul. You can't get people to do something they are not committed to doing for themselves.

I have to admit that writing all of this made me feel really sad—pathetic, even. But mostly sad. I have read and listened to enough of Brené Brown's advice to know that I shouldn't shame myself for being human. Being human is, in fact, the goal.

As it turns out, I was not Superwoman; I was "only" human. A human with feelings and thoughts and wants and needs. A human with limits and boundaries. A human who can tell people, "No!" (Gasp!) A human who is important because she is human, not because she is Superwoman.

ACHIEVEMENT ADDICTION IS a unique form of addiction. Unlike being addicted to alcohol or a drug, you can't just stop achieving. You need to achieve, even in small ways, every single day. You need to keep a job, keep your kids safe and healthy, and have relationships with others. You can't just stop achieving like you can stop shooting up or going to a bar. I'm not saying it's harder; it's just different.

So how do you "cure" an achievement addiction? Like most addictions, you don't; you simply learn how to manage it. For me, that meant doing the hard work of getting to know myself for the first time. Learning what made me happy, sad, or angry. Allowing myself to experience those emotions. Communicating my feelings or needs to others. Setting boundaries and loving myself.

This is why I started my story the way I did; it's those seemingly mundane or silly things, such as sharing my love of hats (actual ones), that I want you to take away as special about me. I now have the benefit of a few years of getting to know myself and I have found that I enjoy being silly sometimes.

WHILE I STILL FEEL "good" when I am succeeding at work or in life, my "why" is much different today. I am a full-time single mom of three, ages 2, 3, and 5; a three-nights-a-week bonus mom to three other children, ages 3, 5, and 8; and a very long distance bonus mom to a 14-year-old.

I am chef, chauffeur, boo-boo fixer, lunch maker, problem solver, cockroach killer, fish feeder, house cleaner, and probably 30 other things that most of you can relate to and share.

I am the Deputy General Counsel of a company that designs and mass manufactures satellites for low earth orbit—a #SpaceLawyer. In non-COVID times, I am on the road at least one full week per month.

I am an adjunct professor at the University of Miami School of Law. I am a mentor, a blogger, and an entrepreneur. I created a company during the pandemic, but it wasn't the first I had launched.

I am a partner to a man who loves me for who I am. Let me tell you how frustrating that is sometimes. I find that I look for praise and adoration within my relationship, things I have primarily stopped searching for in the rest of my life. My man is proud of me, don't get me wrong, but he is largely unimpressed or unfazed by my big legal career. He only marginally cares that I can balance 642 spinning plates at a time, all with a smile on my face. He just loves me—the complicated parts, the imperfections, the emotions, the never-ending thoughts, the nerdiness, and the heart. It's an incredible gift and incredibly frustrating; yet I love him more for it every single day.

Each "hat" that I wear is a part of me, but not one hat epitomizes me. Today, I am "just" a Superwoman in recovery; a woman who has come to the realization that I do not have to do everything for anyone, let alone everyone, particularly at the sacrifice of my own hopes, dreams, and plans. That doesn't make me any less extraordinary; it makes me human.

Thanks for reading my story. I hope I have been able to inspire you to be your most authentic self. And even more so ... to be human.

CHAPTER EIGHTEEN

The Parenting Lawyer

by Lisa Quinn O'Flaherty

> *"Parenting causes smart lawyers to refocus and to be the change they want to see. I spend more time looking for productive ways to work, and less time fretting over the small things. Things change but commitment to a legal vocation remains the same."*

I'M GRATEFUL FOR THE opportunity to share my experiences as a lawyer who is a mother, and the impact of parenting on my studies and my career. My aim is to encourage parents—mothers in particular—to overcome any hesitation to embark on the legal path, safe in the knowledge that legal careers can lend themselves to work-family balance. I also want to share some of the things I have learnt along my journey.

My law school experience was a little bit unconventional, as I was already parenting. I had a very different outlook on life than my classmates. I was lucky enough to have the opportunity to attend night classes three nights a week during term time, and I worked during the day. My wonderfully supportive parents helped with childcare, and as a result, they have a beautifully close relationship with my eldest boy. A support network, wherever it can be found, is vital for parenting—particularly for parenting while being a student.

At times, I felt a bit left behind when classmates applied for summer internships and enhanced their curriculum vitae by participating in legal competitions, work shadowing, and taking additional courses. I did not have the time for these extra-curricular activities; I simply could not quit my paying job to take a summer internship.

I compensated by taking additional online courses on every legal topic imaginable—staying up late at night and getting up early in the mornings to log on. I read law texts and was determined to achieve excellent academics. I sought out opportunities to learn more and to put learning into practice. I followed experienced colleagues on LinkedIn and discovered the things they were interested in. I focussed on the things that were within my control and could help me stand out.

Exam times and assignment times were quite challenging; I watched others just clear their schedules and create blocks of time to study. I learned to start preparing early. I would attend all lectures and take good notes to be exam ready without the need for too much cramming. With a small child, every day involves competing demands on your time and energy; an impending exam is just another demand and needs to find its place on the list of priorities.

I did not have much time for socialising, as you can imagine. One of the biggest sacrifices I had to make was building new friendships and developing old ones. As my legal career has developed, I have learned to balance social connections more productively. Most of my closest friends are people with whom I spend time volunteering in community organisations. And since living with COVID restrictions, I have learnt that a walk in the park can combine exercise, fresh air, and quality time with a friend.

PARENTING PREPARES A PERSON for looking at the big picture and focusing on the key issues. It is a crash course in organisation and planning. I transferred these skills to my studies. I looked at legal topics strategically. I analysed past exam papers early and focussed on the important things.

Parenting provides motivation and drive; when meeting other students who are parents, I got an overwhelming sense that once they have committed to a legal career, they will work their hardest. When a person is sacrificing quality time with their children, they are not going to half-heartedly study. They are goal-focussed and will show commitment and resilience in achieving it.

Adaptability and problem-solving are other parenting skills that translate well to a career in law. Parents are constantly making changes to their schedules and seeking solutions; plans detailed months ago can be derailed by a rash or a bad night's sleep. Disappointment needs to be mitigated and alternative plans made at short notice.

Anyone with a toddler will become expert in negotiation very quickly; no class in collaborative practice can prepare you to persuade a hysterical 2-year-old that an ice cream sundae is not an appropriate breakfast. Problem-solving parents learn that sometimes a small scoop of vanilla on a bowl of porridge can meet everyone's need to get the day started without tears or hunger! Parenting lawyers are experts in choosing their battles and judging when to compromise.

I HAVE ALWAYS FOUND the concept of time-management to be elusive. There are 24 hours in a day, and there is no negotiating this fact. We do not manage time; we manage our priorities. There will always be a trade-off. This trade-off requires a clear sight of priorities and discipline. Students who are parenting must prioritise study over other things like socialising, fitness, and recreation. I found it helpful to keep sight of the important things—the items that were getting my attention—rather than focusing on what was being missed.

It is also important to remember that the fluctuations of life will cause your priorities to constantly be in flux; but the sacrifices are not permanent. During the lead up to my Law Society entrance exams, my husband took our son on adventures every Saturday to give me time to study in peace at home. It pained my heart to miss out on that quality time; but once those exams were over, I never again took for granted the blank slate of a whole Saturday. We have been on more family adventures than you can imagine!

ONE KEY PIECE OF advice for any aspiring lawyer is to find a mentor, someone who sees your strengths better than you do. This person does not need to be on the exact legal trajectory as you envision for yourself, but they need to know the legal world enough to point you in the right direction.

My mentor came in the form of my thesis supervisor, Barry, a truly wonderful person who encouraged me to believe in myself through a combination of gentle nudges and blunt pushes. He would debate law and politics with me, often playing devil's advocate, to help me develop my arguments and debate skills; and he took pleasure in the rare occasions when I would win the debate. I still wish that there was opportunity for him to teach me a fraction of everything he knew; alas, his untimely death occurred just two months before I qualified as a solicitor.

It was with Barry's guidance that I began to picture the shape that I wanted my career to take. I watched with a little envy as classmates endured the arduous application process of the "top" firms; those with prestige and high trainee salaries! I knew that the expectation in those firms was long hours and a commitment to teamwork that involved Friday night drinks with the department and teambuilding trips. I also knew that to start in such a firm would be to embark on a journey—starting as a trainee then graduating to solicitor, then on to associate, senior associate, and eventually partner. The journey would require making work the number-one priority and a never-ending goal to achieve more. The typical journey of a lawyer is not one that lends itself to prioritizing family in the early years.

LEARNING WHAT I DIDN'T want was an important step and perhaps the easiest step in determining what I wanted my career to be. Not having taken the same route as many of my classmates while in law school, I found that a lack of in-office experience somewhat limited my calls to interview. When I landed my first interview, I wasn't sure whether to broach the subject of being a parent; but I decided to be open and honest. I spoke about the skills that parenting develops and how I would apply them in the legal environment. I must've done a great job of translating my parenting skills to the practice of law because I got the job.

Was the job a perfect fit for me? No. Was it in an area of law in which I had a particular interest? No. But it was an "in" to the legal world, and I was very happy to compromise. It was a very raw area of law, and as a junior person, I was exposed to quite a bit of responsibility without much guidance. This led to a phenomenally fast learning experience. After about a year and a half, I felt I had enough experience under my belt to seek out a job in an office more suited to the path I wanted my career to take.

My exposure to the legal world gave me greater confidence and competence, and the vital experience that I needed to chase the type of role I wanted. I was better able to define my own idea of success. I decided that I wanted to work in a mature, smaller firm. I wanted to be building relationships with clients and exceeding their expectations. I wanted the opportunity to develop skills in different practice areas and be able to jump between different tasks.

I interviewed at Fitzsimons Redmond and immediately got a good feeling. There was clear respect among colleagues and the principal, John, who was straight-talking and calm. At the same time, I was also at the second interview stage with another firm. The work was broadly similar, but the attitudes and atmosphere were vastly different. The other firm was talking about pressure, deadlines, and competitiveness; John was talking about client satisfaction, building trust, and flexibility. I kept my fingers crossed for a call-back from him and was delighted to accept the offer when it came a week later.

I wanted my career to work around my family; but I also understood that there are times when work comes first, and I am not against the occasional late night or weekend spent in the office. However, in my work, this is a rarity. Fitzsimons Redmond LLP values wellness, which means we have a culture of being prepared. We focus on the long picture and are picky about the cases that we take on. We avoid panic and are solution focussed. When things get challenging, John has always been there with both practical and moral support. His calm demeanor brings balance to the whole office.

AT SOME POINT, I found myself questioning the trajectory of my career. I began wondering whether I should seek out a role in a larger firm. The idea of moving to another firm did not appeal to me, but I had to question whether I was becoming too comfortable. Then I took a step back and looked at my work. I realized that my work constantly exposes me to new challenges, and I am given the scope to make my role what I want it to be. I asked myself, "Isn't this exactly what you wanted for your legal career?" My answer was a resounding yes!

Fitzsimons Redmond LLP is a people-focused firm, where leadership can flourish. Leadership is more than managing people and mentoring junior colleagues; it involves modelling healthy work-life balance behaviours while embracing change and championing ideas and values that will improve the workplace.

I have found that in a healthy work environment, there are endless opportunities for leadership prior to gaining any formal leadership role. In my firm, I became the champion of the Law Society's Wellness Charter, which promotes healthy working practices, in particular a respect for colleagues' right to disconnect. The values of the Wellness Charter are firmly ingrained in the values of Fitzsimons Redmond LLP, and we needed to implement very few changes when we became a signatory. But I felt it was important that we show our commitment to healthy working practices so as to normalise it in the working world. As a working mother, I believe I am a model for healthy working practices.

At Fitzsimons Redmond LLP, I have freedom to develop in ways that I want to. I hugely value lifelong learning and am usually studying one course or another. I can bring my learnings and interests into the workplace, developing and expanding practice areas. I see the successes of our firm as being my own successes, and these have always been recognised and encouraged at Fitzsimons Redmond LLP. Being recently appointed a partner, I find that as the firm makes an upward and outward trajectory, my own career travels with it. There are no real limits on what we can achieve.

IN LIFE, THERE ARE times where career is the focus, and times where family is; the goal is to have these ebbs and flows go smoothly and not feel as though one aspect is neglected as the other takes centre stage. The huge advantage of working in such a supportive environment is that I never felt I had to give up on any career move when we decided to try for another baby.

I took six months of maternity leave when my youngest was born (which is the standard leave in Ireland), but I never felt any diversion from my career path. In fact, I feel lucky that when I returned to the office, I had the opportunity to choose my own working hours—starting very early in the morning and finishing up by early afternoon. I discovered that this was a very productive way for me to work; I get a huge amount of drafting done and opinions written early in the day when I am fresh and free from distractions. I can do my communication work at an appropriate hour while feeling happy that I have morning's work behind me. The ability to schedule emails allows me to respect the conventional working hours of others while getting tasks off my desk.

I am lucky to work in a firm that is open to new ideas and supportive of initiatives that improve our working lives. Our firm was among the first signatories to The Law Society of Ireland's Charter on Gender Equality, Diversity, and Inclusion and the Charter on Workplace Wellness. When I introduced the firm to the idea of signing, there was unanimous support for all the principles enshrined in both charters. There is a certain degree of overlap in the values, in that where healthy working practices are valued, inclusion becomes more attainable.

WHEN I RETURNED FROM my last maternity leave, I negotiated a four-day working week with no loss of salary. I gained an extra day of family time; a day to go for walks with friends and introduce my baby to other babies (although harshly limited by COVID). I felt valued and appreciated at work. My employer was safe in the knowledge that I possessed the dedication required to perform my job in its entirety in four days. Importantly, I was also testing the idea to see if a shorter workweek could be rolled out to the entire office while searching for strategies to maintain productivity.

The four-day week phenomenon is very interesting—with global studies showing that workers are equally productive in four days as they are in five. It is a model that works very well for parents who would like more time with their children, and those who face high childcare costs (a real issue in Ireland where the cost of childcare for two children can equal half of a family's income). It is also a model that works well for people with disabilities where recovery time after the working week can be longer, and for people who are coming up to retirement and want to enjoy more free time. In fact, there are very few workers who wouldn't benefit from a shorter workweek. It is for those reasons Fitzsimons Redmond LLP is now the first law firm in Ireland to introduce the four-day week as its policy.

TO ALL ASPIRING COLLEAGUES, know yourself; put yourself in situations that challenge you and learn about your own true values. My experiences have taught me that I value family, making the world a better place, and personal development. Once I identified my own values, I gained the ability to surround myself with people I admire. I have learnt so much—and grown so much—while watching wonderful people approach challenges in different ways. I have been able to model the admirable behaviours of my husband, my parents, my partner at Fitzsimons Redmond LLP, the people with whom I volunteer, and some very dear friends, all of whom have brought improvements to my life.

Know that firms with healthy, family-friendly values are not unicorns, and that sometimes it takes your own leadership to bring policies to the next level. Never be afraid to step up and propose inclusive working practices where you think it will improve the workplace for you and for others.

Always be learning and always be open to new challenges. With new knowledge comes new confidence—and new perspective. I always like to be learning and am willing to sacrifice other things (such as television shows in the evenings) to learn things that will help me grow as a professional. I don't limit my learnings to legal topics or formal study; I spend time volunteering with charities and community organisations. I like to look at new ways to upskill in order to bring value to clients. Through study and volunteering, I have developed networking opportunities without spending time on the golf course.

It has been said that parenting can make lawyers lose focus on their work; my lived experience is not a loss of focus, but rather a refocus. Parenting causes smart lawyers to refocus and to be the change they want to see. I spend more time looking for productive ways to work, and less time fretting over the small things. Things change but commitment to a legal vocation remains the same.

Parenting does not make us less committed; it makes us see with clarity the end goal. We will work efficiently to meet that goal, using the countless skills that we are honing at home every single day!

CHAPTER NINETEEN

I Am an Anomaly

by Suzie Smith

> *"I think it's important for women, mothers—hell, anyone—to know that you can be faced with all sorts of impediments and still be successful. You can and will overcome. You don't have to be an anomaly to find your inner strength. You don't have to be unique. All you have to be is determined and willing to do more in order to get more."*

I HAVE BEEN AN ANOMALY for my entire existence. The anomalous character of my being began in my mother's womb. When my mother was carrying me, she miscarried. The diagnosis at the time was spontaneous twin abortion. Her doctors put her on bedrest and she later gave birth to a lone baby girl.

After my birth, I went nameless until my parents were told my birth certificate needed a name. The original plan was to name me Joseph Paul (my dad's name is Paul) because my parents thought I was going to be a boy. They could not agree on a name for a girl. My dad's father disliked the name Emma, and even Emily was out of the question unless it could be used as a middle name or that I could be referred to by a middle name. Eventually, they settled on Emily Susan, but I had to be referred to as "Suzie." Ironically, I love the name Suzie and identify with it even more than with Emily or Susan; though I briefly tried out Emily and "Em" for a short time.

AS YOU MAY HAVE noticed by now, I grew up in a dysfunctional household. My father was abusive; later, my parents divorced. This experience led me to make some poor choices, including marrying an abusive spouse. My father (who is different now) spent my youth constantly reminding me of how worthless and stupid I was. In high school, I didn't value knowledge because I didn't know the gifts I had. All I knew was what I was told by the people in my life.

I dropped out of high school, got married at a young age, and had two children by the time I was 21. After nine years of marriage, I filed for divorce. I already had begun working on a two-year degree but had to put my studies on hold through the divorce. With two young children in tow, I did what I had to do in order to survive—I took a position with a pizza place for a short time during my divorce. Unfortunately, that job ended abruptly after the owner tried to whip my rear end with a towel while I was working.

When my current spouse and I began living together, I was struggling to find good employment. At the time, I had only completed a semester of my associate's degree but was frequently told I was overqualified. As a child, I had always dreamed of having a "fancy" professional job; but I never thought it would happen. My husband suggested that I finish my degree. He offered unfettered support as I struggled to get back on track, facing a bevy of obstacles.

For example, we live in the middle of nowhere and didn't even have internet at the time. I had to email documents to the school as part of the application process, and the closest location that offered public computers was a library in a town five miles from where we live. But I was determined to let nothing get in my way. I had faced obstacles before and this was clearly a surmountable one. So my daughters and I jumped on our bicycles and rode them to town. This was quite the feat for someone who had never really ridden a bike, and even more so for my girls who were only 7 and 8 years old at the time.

WHILE WORKING TO OBTAIN my associate's degree, I got pregnant with our fifth child. Gary had two girls from a previous relationship and I had my two girls. Then we added another girl to our blended family.

Getting pregnant and having a child could have easily derailed my progress as a full-time student. But I refused to allow it. I found the strength to continue and took 18 credit hours each semester to finish as quickly as possible. It took me roughly a year and a half to get my associate's degree.

I graduated with a 3.6 GPA, yet on the day of my graduation, I felt unsatisfied. I felt under-accomplished. Our youngest daughter was still nursing and had gone much of the day without her mother. She immediately wanted to nurse before we went home. I nursed her while still wearing my graduation gown. She then proceeded to throw up all over me. The ride home covered in baby vomit encapsulated my feelings for the day.

I spent the next couple of weeks attempting to find employment that would allow me to work at home and be with our youngest daughter. When nothing availed itself, I decided to pursue my bachelor's degree. Unfortunately, at that time, online options for non-traditional students were few and far between. The two schools that made it to the finals were Liberty University (which I eventually settled on) and a school in Maryland that offered online programs in my field of study.

I started working on my bachelor's degree in June and finished the following July. Again, I found myself unsatisfied with even my latest accomplishment—even after earning a 3.9 GPA! There was something missing. I wanted more—not only for me but for my family. I had considered pursuing a degree in paralegal studies, but I wasn't sure that being a paralegal would be financially secure enough for a family of seven. That's when I told my husband I wanted to go to law school. His initial reaction was unexpected; in fact, I found his laughter offensive. He then explained that his laughter was in anticipation of the fact that I wouldn't be satisfied with what I had accomplished thus far and would want to keep going.

For two and a half years, I would drop off our youngest at pre-school and drive an hour to and from law school. I was much older than my law school peers; so making friends was challenging at first. It made me think I had made the wrong decision. Then I met a group of students with similar interests and we hit it off.

ALTHOUGH I DID NOT graduate from law school at the top of my class, the kid who was told she was "stupid" and "worthless" passed the bar on the first try. (Wahoo!) While in school, I had been lucky enough to land a job as a law clerk for a general practice law firm in my county. Soon after passing the bar, I was offered a full-time position as an associate. The work allows me the opportunity to experience a variety of cases—family law, business, minor criminal, estate planning, etc.—while assisting the firm's partners with municipal work, which is a firm specialty.

As a high school dropout, I have always carried with me a feeling of failure. My need to achieve most likely stems from an inner desire to prove to myself that I am more than the labels others had always placed on me. I grew up hearing constantly how much of a disappointment I was. When I chose law school, I was looking for a way to feel accomplished but I wasn't sure if law school would actually provide me with that. By happenstance, learning the foundations of law and our civil rights and the ways the law has oppressed certain people have been the most satisfying for me. I never would have gained that knowledge where I live, which is primarily rural and rampant with white privilege and latent racism. I now feel equipped with the tools to help others while feeling financially capable of helping myself and my family.

I WAS BORN AN ANOMALY, and I still consider myself one—but in the most positive way. Being an anomaly makes me unique. I now realize that my anomalous existence also makes me special. I didn't always see my life this way; and because of that, I made some poor choices.

God is my number-one credit, but my number two is the desire I have to stop limiting my life based on labels someone else attempts to place on me. I allowed those labels to place me in a box; once trapped, I would use those labels as a reason not to do things, or to do things that weren't good for me. The limitations I placed on myself kept me from going after more. But once I realized how capable I was, I was determined to never let labels stop me again.

I have faced numerous obstacles in my life: having two children by the age of 21; marrying someone who was abusive and who struggled with addiction; dropping out of high school—these aren't things that a young woman with a healthy self-esteem would do.

But once I stepped away from what everyone else saw, I was able to set goals for myself and believe that I could achieve them.

And what is life without its obstacles? In January 2020, I became ill. Looking back, I suspect it was COVID-19 but testing didn't exist at that time. In March of the same year, I got shingles. The following July, I got shingles again; and if not for being totally unlucky, I officially contracted COVID-19 in November. These bouts of illness have caused disruptions to my work and hobbies; unfortunately, they come with lingering symptoms. But just as I have overcome other obstacles in my life that I once viewed as insuperable, this, too, shall pass.

I think it's important for women, mothers—hell, anyone—to know that you can be faced with all sorts of impediments and still be successful. You can and will overcome. You don't have to be an anomaly to find your inner strength. You don't have to be unique. All you have to be is determined and willing to do more in order to get more.

Create your own labels. See yourself for who you really are.

CHAPTER TWENTY

Build Your Own Ladder

by Jamie Sternberg

"Each rung in the ladder of my career has taken me to a higher degree of confidence, fulfillment, curiosity, and skill."

WHEN NON-LAWYERS, law students, and lawyers think of what it is to be a successful lawyer, a few common themes come to mind—going to an Ivy League school, graduating at the top of your class, joining a top-tier law firm, becoming a partner, being a rainmaker, winning cases, surpassing the billable hour requirement, earning a lot of money, and receiving honors and awards.

This is what you see in the movies, on television, on LinkedIn, and this is what may be encouraged at some law firms. While there is no doubt that any one of these factors demonstrates success, success and fulfillment as an attorney can be defined in many ways.

When I decided to go to law school, I had no idea what success would mean as a lawyer. In the summer of 2000, I was going into my senior year of college at Tufts University, outside of Boston. I was majoring in Political Science and minoring in English. The perfect recipe to become a lawyer, right? But that is the path my older sister and brother took, so I needed to do something different. I decided to explore a career in advertising and marketing like my dad. Somehow, I managed to snag a summer internship in the marketing department at Monster.com, one of the dot-com phenoms of the day, with an office in Maynard, MA, a short drive away.

I started my internship upon returning to the United States after four months of studying abroad in Tel Aviv, Israel. A few friends and I rented an off-campus apartment on the bottom floor of a two-family house in Somerville, MA, right across the street from the campus Tufts University. It was a 15-minute walk from the Davis "T" subway stop, and I finally had a car at school and street parking.

I no longer had to rely on campus dining halls; we could cook dinner in our own kitchen. We could have our own parties, with our own beer pong table where we'd keep a cup of water to wash the ping pong balls that inevitably bounced onto the dusty, dirty basement floor. And I could sit on any one of the many couches stuffed into the family room and onto the porch by previous renters.

Every morning, I commuted to my internship in the opposite direction of the usual flow of traffic into Boston. I had my car windows open on the highway due to the lack of air conditioning in my Ford Taurus station wagon, typically with a CD of Dave Matthews Band, Coldplay, or Guster blasting through the speakers.

I loved arriving at an office building every day; it included just what you would imagine a successful dot-com company would have: a massive common area with free breakfast, snacks, and lunch options, a ping pong table, larger-than-life purple monster designs on the walls, and an open floor plan. I remember walking through the twisty brick hallways of the old mill building where the office resided to meet my team members for lunch in the cafeteria downstairs. Though I don't recall the details of my work in the marketing department after more than 20 years, I remember a defining moment that placed me on the path to becoming a lawyer.

I was shadowing a member of the marketing department as she went about her duties. She wrote press releases and was dealing with the issue of another job search site misappropriating content from Monster.com's website. We visited the in-house counsel to discuss this matter and I remember wanting to stay there so that I could shadow the counsel as she dealt with this issue.

At the same time, the music downloading service, Napster, was all the rage. While I was studying in Israel, Metallica initiated the first copyright infringement lawsuit against Napster in March 2000. The legal issues surrounding this service intrigued me.

As a result of these experiences, I became fascinated with intellectual property law, in particular, copyright and trademark law. Before my internship at Monster.com concluded in December 2000, I had decided to go to law school. I made a plan to take the year off after I graduated to study for the LSAT, to apply to law schools, and to earn some money.

My ability to take the actions I needed to determine my path after graduation—such as obtaining an internship, exploring my interests, and making a plan—is one of the first markers of success in my legal career. In addition, knowing that I was interested in becoming a trademark and copyright attorney allowed me to focus on applying to schools that would help me further that goal.

I ATTENDED A TOP law school for intellectual property law— Franklin Pierce Law Center, now known as University of New Hampshire Franklin Pierce School of Law (UNH). While it may be impressive that I graduated among the top students in my class, even more valuable was the fact that this school provided me with the foundation I needed to enjoy a successful and fulfilling career as an intellectual property attorney. It offered specialized trademark, copyright, entertainment, and intellectual property law classes and encouraged me to seek an externship.

An apparel and footwear company gave me the opportunity to do an externship in its legal department during the spring semester of my second year. It was here that I received my first taste of practicing in the areas of trademark and copyright law, as well as being part of an in-house legal team. This externship combined with my education at UNH Law, and my ability to make connections, led to my first legal clerk position at a law firm and my first attorney position at the same firm. The practical experience I gained from my law classes and my externship was invaluable and led to a successful legal career.

BUT NO ATTORNEY HAS a legal career without stumbles—and mine is no different. It is through the practice of law that attorneys learn how to be lawyers, to navigate internal politics, to provide client service, to build a practice, and to determine the path they want to follow.

After graduation, I had two job offers: one as a contract attorney at the general practice firm where I had been clerking through my third year of school, and one as an associate at a business-focused firm. At the time, there were very few women at one firm and the other was a known quantity. I decided to go with the known quantity. The firm I chose did not specialize in intellectual property law; but this firm taught me how to be a lawyer.

One of the firm's partners would supervise me when I had the opportunity to work on intellectual property cases. I knew about as much as, or more than, he did. This attorney was my first mentor, my first teacher in the real world of law, my first cheerleader, the first attorney to give me frank criticism, and my first reference after I left. One of the crucial elements of having a successful legal career is finding mentors along the way.

I am grateful that my first job after law school gave me a background in many areas of law—criminal defense, insurance defense, employment law, construction law, white collar crime, property law, and commercial law. It also offered me countless opportunities to attend status conferences and hearings in state courts all over New Hampshire, which I never expected to do, and I was nervous as hell. Apparently, I conveyed this nervousness to others around the office because my mentor sat me down one day and told me to start attending Toastmasters International meetings.

Toastmasters is an international public speaking organization with chapters all over the world. I fell in love with this organization and continued to participate even after I left this firm. I encourage all law students to participate in moot court while in law school; and if you have a fear of public speaking or want to improve your skills, find your local Toastmasters chapter. Learning how to speak confidently to your colleagues, in court, or otherwise is a crucial step toward success as a lawyer.

ONE DAY WHILE SITTING in my office, I received a call from a recruiter about a job in the thriving intellectual property practice group of a large general practice firm in a neighboring state. Just as I never expected to attend court as a practicing attorney, I never expected to practice in this state.

This firm is where I learned how to be an intellectual property attorney, an associate, and the type of attorney who I aspired to be. It is also where I learned to navigate reviews, a billable hour requirement, constructive criticism, and office politics.

My time in this part of the country was one of the best in my life. For the first time, I lived by myself. I rented the second story of a two-family house within walking distance to downtown, to the lake, and to the bike path that runs the length of the lake. I became good friends with the owners of the house who lived downstairs.

I continued attending Toastmasters meetings and am friends with members I met there to this day. I became dedicated to a yoga practice. I enjoyed brunches, dinners, drinking, and dancing. I attended monthly "stitch-and-bitch" sessions with my friends where we pretended to knit, but drank wine instead; and I spent a lot of time with my now husband who lived in another state and came to visit me at what he called his "weekend home."

On days when it was still light after work, I would take runs and bike rides on the bike path. These excursions, my yoga practice, and my friendships outside of work were crucial to my success at the firm. As a junior associate, the years I spent at this firm were transitional. I asked questions (so many questions) before I tried to find answers myself, received a lot of feedback, did not meet the billable hour requirement every year, learned how to prioritize work among the partners, and discovered a lot about myself as an attorney in annual reviews. These valuable experiences contributed to who I am today as a lawyer, supervisor, mentor, and avid note taker.

At this firm, I continued to hone my litigation skills and learned how to prosecute trademark and copyright applications with the U.S. Patent and Trademark Office and the U.S. Copyright Office. I wrote agreements pertaining to patents, trademarks, and copyrights, and handled domain name infringement disputes. I worked with clients who had worldwide trademark portfolios.

My time at this firm set the foundation for my success as an intellectual property attorney. I established relationships with clients that remain today, and solidified friendships with attorneys with whom I still share referrals.

MY FIANCÉ RELOCATED TO my home state after he landed a job there and I transitioned my practice to a large general practice firm with a significant intellectual property group. This is the firm where I got to work with a legend in the field of intellectual property law on a trademark infringement case that now appears in law school textbooks. As a mid-level associate, I had more responsibility, independence, and confidence in my practice, and the means to buy a house on the beautiful, leafy street where I grew up. My now husband and I were the youngest couple by far, with the nicest neighbors in the world, and a house with too many bedrooms. Little did we know that all those rooms would eventually fill up with three kids and two work-from-home offices.

When an opportunity to work for a boutique intellectual property firm arose, I accepted the job and moved my practice across town where I stayed for many years. This is the firm where I learned how to be a working mom; I became a respected trademark attorney in my own right, met a network of international trademark attorneys, and focused deeply on client service.

A trademark attorney licensed in at least one state in the United States can work with clients from all over the country and the world to register trademarks with the U.S. Patent and Trademark Office, to make sure trademarks are available to be used and registered by businesses, to enforce and defend trademark rights before the Trademark Trial and Appeal Board, and to advise on trademark enforcement and registration strategy. While at this firm, I dealt with hundreds of U.S. trademark applications and registrations, managed and enforced numerous trademarks worldwide, and continued to build my Internet enforcement practice.

More than half my practice involved working with law firms located outside of the United States to search, register, and enforce trademarks for their clients in the United States. We, in turn, worked with lawyers all over the world to assist our clients with the same tasks. As a result, I grew a trusted network of colleagues and lifelong friends from all over the world. I had the opportunity to travel all over the United States and the world to meet with clients and attend International Trademark Association conferences. If you ask me to name an intellectual property law firm or attorney who serves a particular country, I can probably name at least one.

During this time, I became a mom to three children. At one point, I grew too big to fit behind my desk and steering wheel when I was carrying my twins. I learned how to navigate motherhood, multiple maternity leaves, and daycare. My firm allowed attorneys to work from home and have reduced hours. As a result, I was able to attend to my responsibilities and interests at home while still managing clients, receiving a promotion, continuing my career trajectory, and staying true to myself.

A couple of years ago, I had the privilege of joining a smaller trademark and copyright firm run by alumni from my law school. This is the firm where I learned to build a practice of my own, to build a referral network, to market, and to make an impact. About eight months before it became the norm to work from home during the pandemic, I worked from home full time and traveled to the office in a neighboring state once a month. I haven't seen my colleagues in person since February 2020. Since we already had the infrastructure in place for remote working, the transition to a remote firm in March 2020 during the pandemic was seamless. The ability to collaborate over Slack messenger and Zoom calls has been crucial to our continued success. In the time I have been here, our team has almost doubled in size.

THE CONFINES OF MY professional box have expanded in extraordinary ways over the past two years in terms of complexity of work, putting myself out there, contributing to firm policy, building a practice, and mentoring. I have met more professionals, business owners, and entrepreneurs in my local area than in the almost decade since we purchased our home. I routinely speak and write nationally and internationally on trademark issues, and am humbled to do that at the request of others. My role as trusted advisor to law firms and businesses has become one of the most meaningful aspects of my life.

Each rung in the ladder of my career has taken me to a higher degree of confidence, fulfillment, curiosity, and skill. Each rung has taken me closer to the attorney, advisor, mentor, wife, mom, and person I aspired to be when I first set out on this path during my senior year of college. I cannot imagine success being defined in any other way.

As you climb, consider the following factors that contributed to my success:

- ❖ Be yourself.
- ❖ Find an area of the law you are passionate about.
- ❖ Build relationships.
- ❖ Learn how to give and receive constructive criticism with grace.

- ❖ Listen.

- ❖ Take notes.

- ❖ Find answers before asking someone else.

- ❖ Become skillful at navigating different personalities and law firm policies.

- ❖ Understand when to back down and when to push back.

- ❖ Be a nice person.

- ❖ Take initiative.

- ❖ Be a team player.

- ❖ Manage your time.

- ❖ Take the time to rest and reset.

- ❖ Work independently.

- ❖ Think before you act.

- ❖ Take a deep breath, walk away, or sleep on it.

- ❖ Be a mentor.

- ❖ Make client service number one.

- ❖ Work with a coach.

- ❖ Network.

- ❖ Build your own practice.

- ❖ Stay current on the law.

- ❖ Share your knowledge.

- ❖ Remain curious.

- ❖ Keep learning from your colleagues.

Get out from behind your desk and get outside of your box.

CHAPTER TWENTY-ONE

A Less Traditional Path

by Heather Stevenson

> *"One could say that I have life figured out. Of course, that wouldn't be true. Life can't be 'figured out.' What I want and need, and what works for my family, are constantly evolving."*

I QUIT MY JOB AS a litigation associate at a top international firm in order to open a juice bar.

Sounds like a joke, doesn't it? But I'm totally serious.

That decision defined and shaped my career in ways that were both expected and totally surprising, and it set me on the path to success as a lawyer—the path I am still on today.

Leaving the practice of law helped me redefine what success looks like for me, and it helped me unwind my self-worth from my identity as a lawyer. I learned that the most important part of the oft-repeated phrase, "you can be whatever you want to be," is the part about doing what I want and being who I want to be and not—as I had previously assumed—simply following the expectations that others have placed on me based on the career goals they aspired to. I choose to be a mom, wife, friend, lawyer, advocate for justice, a runner, a food lover, and many other identities. And I am allowed to change my identities, or how I express them, whenever I want.

But let me take a step back.

My parents both spent their careers as BigLaw partners. I don't recall anyone ever referring to it as "BigLaw" back in the 1990s, but that's what it was. They worked a lot. They were great at their jobs. And they enjoyed what they did. Dad was quiet and contemplative by nature. He was a talented real estate lawyer well-regarded by all who knew him or his work. He chose to retire while I was still in high school and continues to enjoy retirement just as much as he enjoyed practicing. Mom, whose personality is the opposite of Dad's, is a high energy, social by nature trial lawyer who is still practicing. She loves what she does and says she plans to keep working until that changes. From wearing her brown hair short with gold spikes, to painting the walls of her "white shoe" law firm office pink, she has insisted on doing things her own way for as long as I can remember.

Mom and I look a lot alike and we have some similar personality traits. So it's not especially surprising that ever since my preschool days, people predicted I would one day be a lawyer "just like Mom."

Growing up, I experienced the benefits of being the daughter of two successful lawyers—living in a wonderful town, attending great schools, enjoying fantastic family vacations, etc., etc. I liked having lawyers for parents and benefited immensely—not only from the tangible benefits, but also from watching my parents dedicate themselves to work they cared deeply about. Though the lawyer meme is of an over-worked father who routinely misses bedtime and birthday parties, and a conflicted mother who never manages to be either the mother or the lawyer she intends to be, that was not my family's experience. Neither of my parents ever missed my birthday. My best friend and I regularly spent weekday afternoons after sports practice in Mom's law firm office and we thought it was great fun. And while Mom's Blackberry made frequent appearances at my skating lessons, tennis tournaments, and even half way up Mt. Kilimanjaro during a family vacation, I always knew I was more important to her than her Blackberry was.

With all this working in my favor, it seemed almost preordained that—if I wanted to—I could become a lawyer, too. Though I considered other paths, and at various times vigorously proclaimed that I would never be a lawyer, deep down, I think I always assumed I would.

I GRADUATED FROM Columbia College in 2006 and joined Teach for America as a sixth grade English Language Arts and Social Studies teacher in the South Bronx. In 2008, after two years as a corps member, I returned to Columbia for law school. Having always enjoyed learning, I liked law school a lot. I thought my professors were brilliant, my classmates were wonderful (and not nearly as competitive as I had feared), and I had an all-around wonderful time. I capped off my three years spending a semester in Amsterdam and completing my LLM in International Criminal Law while earning my JD.

In 2011, I finally became what everyone thought I would be—a lawyer.

After the bar exam, I joined the New York office of a large international firm where I had worked as a summer associate between my 2L and 3L years. I was assigned to work on a series of mortgage-backed security-related cases as well as some shareholder derivative litigation, most of which were for the same large banking client. I liked my colleagues. I liked working on important cases. I even found shareholder derivative litigation strangely intriguing (no one believes me when I say this, but it's true!).

I settled into law firm life while building routines that worked for me.

Most mornings, I would run from my apartment on the Upper West Side to my office in Lower Manhattan; it was a beautiful seven or so mile run along the Hudson, which allowed me to start my day clear headed. I joined Equinox and used its Wall Street location to shower and get ready for work. This meant, assuming no work "emergencies," I could often spend a few precious minutes in the steam room before showering and getting ready. I kept jackets and work shoes in my office and ran with a backpack.

I typically wouldn't leave the building from the time I arrived around 9:00 am to whatever time I left for home at the end of the day, usually around 9:30 pm. Looking back, I should have gone outside more. But from my first weeks at the firm, I was very busy and too nervous to be away from my desk.

The cases I worked on were huge. Huge money. Huge teams. It was the type of litigation that gets covered in the *Wall Street Journal* and *New York Times*. The law was complex and the facts messy. I did my fair share of document review, as all litigation associates did at the time (I hear machines are coming for our jobs, and when it comes to document review, AI is welcome to it). But I also did work I found challenging and interesting. I attended depositions, drafted dispositive motions, prepared outlines for oral argument, and attended the hearings. Given the size of the cases and that I only stayed with the firm for three years, I covered a great amount of substance. I was largely happy.

Over time, however, when I imagined myself looking back on my career 30 or 40 years into the future, I didn't want my life to have been spent at a firm. Fitting in bits of joy, like my regular runs along the Hudson helped, but it wasn't enough. I was curious about too many things. I was annoyed by the bureaucracy and hierarchical structure. And I despise inefficiency, which is built into both.

I DIDN'T HATE THE LAW. I didn't hate my firm. I didn't hate the work. There was no tearful all-nighter or rage-induced firm-wide email announcing my resignation. I could have continued doing what I was doing for another few years and would've been just fine. At least until we had children, I imagined.

But I wasn't going to settle for "just fine." I wanted to be really excited about the work that I do. And my husband and I had long joked about opening a food business. The joke gradually became a serious idea after we identified a gap in the Boston market for a juice bar. I'm from Boston and my husband had family there, so it made sense.

In 2014, we moved to Boston and opened Thirst Juice Co., a plant-based juice and smoothie bar, in the financial district. That makes it sound simple. It wasn't. The months leading up to our opening were stressful and full of challenges. We had so much to learn. I dealt more in those months with gender discrimination than at any other time in my career. And if law firm hours were long, business owner hours were all-consuming. But I loved it.

In 2016, we opened a second location. I loved building the business and the community we supported, which, in turn, supported us. I loved constantly learning. I loved being my own boss. I could write a chapter just about Thirst; but in a book about lawyers, I'll leave it at this: Building Thirst was an invaluable experience for which I will be forever grateful. And it prepared me to be a much better in-house lawyer than I ever would have been had I transitioned directly from a law firm to in-house.

In August 2017, our son was born and I thought I would run the business while caring for him full-time. That plan worked exactly as well as one would expect. I loved being a mother but did not love being at home all the time, especially while trying to run a business. Plus, I was starting to miss thinking like a lawyer.

IN LATE NOVEMBER 2017, I decided I would take the February Massachusetts bar exam and then try to find a job the following fall, around our son's first birthday. I started looking on LinkedIn® and Indeed® to get a sense of the Boston legal market. Almost immediately, I saw a job that looked really fun and seemed like a great fit. I didn't meet the listed qualifications (law firm transactional work), but from the description of what the job actually entailed, I knew I could do it. The job primarily involved reviewing and negotiating contracts. How many contracts had I negotiated for Thirst? Dozens, hundreds, maybe? I couldn't be sure, but the number was high.

I recently had come across a now well-known study claiming that men apply for jobs when they meet only 60% of the listed qualifications, while women tend to apply only if they meet 100% of the listed qualifications. I thought if a man would apply, I should, too.

The role was Legal Counsel for the parent company of *The Boston Globe*. I had a connection to the General Counsel in charge of hiring, which was enough to get him to talk to me. I applied, met with him, and by the end of December, I had a job offer. I didn't have the experience he had initially imagined would make someone qualified to do the work, but I had different experience that more than adequately prepared me. He hired me even though he knew I wasn't going to immediately shut down Thirst, and even though I had an infant at home. He was willing to take the risk, and I'll always be grateful to him for that. I worked hard to make sure no one would question his decision to hire someone who had taken a less traditional path.

Over the course of the past four years at the *Globe*, my responsibilities have both shifted and drastically expanded. I was promoted to Assistant General Counsel and then to Deputy General Counsel. I am now the legal point person for many of the areas our department covers; and rather than performing basic contract negotiation, I now supervise the lawyer who does. I am the point person for our newsroom on topics ranging from fair use to public records, and I work closely with colleagues across the company and with our executive team on a range of matters.

I GET TO PUT MY SON to bed and have dinner with my husband nearly every night. I run daily. And, weather permitting, I get outside for a few minutes in the middle of every day. We take vacations and never worry whether we'll need to cancel because of work. I don't run the risk of having to spend all day on my laptop instead of exploring with my family.

One could say that I have life figured out. Of course, that wouldn't be true. Life can't be "figured out." What I want and need, and what works for my family, are constantly evolving. I now know that I, and we, can adjust as we go, and that we can change our minds. And for us, knowing we can always pivot to make things better is what success looks like.

Predictions that I would become a lawyer like my mom turned out to be true; yet, I am still not "just like" her. That's the beauty of life as a mom who is also a lawyer, and a lawyer who is also a mom. We each get to decide what works for us and our families.

For anyone who dares to tell us we're doing it wrong, well, I have a thing or two to say about that. And I know dozens of other women who do, too.

CHAPTER TWENTY-TWO

My 'Unquantifiable' Value

by Jamie Szal

It is easy to think that your value lies only in your production. Conceiving of value as something other than numbers takes intention.
It helps to be motivated as well.

MY STORY IS ONE I have been writing for several decades and yet only writing with intention for the last two.

I can tell you all the things I am—listing the facts, as I would say to my daughter. I am a woman. I am a lawyer. I am a wife. I am a mother. I am an eldest child (with all of its stereotypes). I am Sicilian and Irish (and my personality is the best and worst of both). Then there are my intangible features. I am independent. I am intelligent. I am determined.

Yet, what I am is not the same thing as who I am. It was not until I took ownership of my story that I could conceive of what it is that has made my life a success, and what I want that success to continue to mean.

AT SOME POINT DURING the pandemic, a meme floated around social media. Ultra-independence, as the meme reflected, is a by-product of trauma. The point of the meme was that something has happened in our lives to break our reliance on another person, to force us out of community with others, and to depend only on ourselves.

If we are lucky, we have a mentor or, better yet, a champion within our firm. Yet, so often, we are left to fend for ourselves. This is true for so many women who are lawyers, particularly lawyer moms. We are in many ways alone in our worlds. Oftentimes, each of us is the only woman in our practice groups; the only woman at the negotiating table; the only woman in the courtroom. The only woman.

As a result, we develop that ultra-independence. We put our heads down. We work. We have aspirations for ourselves, but have very little support around us to make those aspirations a reality.

Such was my experience when I transitioned from the public sector to the private world. There I was. In a new state. In a new job. Away from family and friends. Away from any support network or safety net. Anxious? You bet. However, this transition represented the first time I dreamed bigger for myself.

I remember two moments during my interviews where that dream began to take shape. I was asked, "What is it about the opportunity that really excites you?" There I sat in front of a lawyer who already had made his name in the SALT (state and local tax) world. I spoke out loud my deep ambition—that the real possibility of working on a U.S. Supreme Court matter was an opportunity I could not pass up. This was beyond the "kid in a candy shop" dream that every 1L harbors. This was the opportunity to be a part of something so much bigger—precedent setting, industry upending. It was the opportunity to be a part of history.

I was more than a bit uncertain about breathing life into that dream, for fear it could never be. Perhaps I manifested some of that uncertainty. Not long after that moment, another attorney asked me, "Are you ready to leave a job you are so admittedly happy with?" I honestly did not know, and said as much. But I also said that I did not see myself remaining a career public servant and I was more excited than I was apprehensive.

In the short term, this new adventure reinforced that "head down focus" drive that my ultra-independence had fostered early in my career. Then not long into this new job came the shock of learning I was pregnant after years of infertility treatments. My reaction was to work longer and harder.

I WAS ALREADY ON my own in so many ways as a professional; looking back, I facilitated my own isolation. I allowed myself to buy into the idea that as the only woman on a busy, in-demand team—much less the one woman who was about to become a mother—I needed to make sure I was seen as a valuable member. It was some time later I realized I needed to take ownership of my own value, which meant that I would have to recognize my value before I could expect anyone else to recognize it.

This was all well and good. But as someone who for years wouldn't dare think big about my own value, and certainly never attempted to quantify it, what the heck did that mean?

As a tax lawyer, I am naturally drawn to numbers. So when I first began to conceive of my value, my mind focused on billables and hourly rates along with quantifiable metrics to show how fiscally valuable I was to my firm. It is easy to get lost in the numbers. Numbers are quantifiable. I could see at a glance: how many hours did I bill? What is my billable rate? What revenue did I generate? How many clients did I bring in? It is easy to think that your value lies only in your productivity. Conceiving value as something other than numbers takes intention. It helps to be motivated as well.

That motivation, for me, has been motherhood.

We did not know what gender our child would be while I was pregnant. I used to joke, "What do you expect me to do? Give the kid back?" While pregnant, my child's gender truly did not make a difference to me. In so many ways, it still is not significant. And yet, discovering that I had given birth to a daughter had a profound effect on me. Suddenly, all of my thoughts coalesced about professional women who are ambitious and have a much-grounded sense of self. It became imperative that I get out of my own head, stop thinking about qualities I wished I could nurture in myself, and set about actually developing those qualities. I needed to be a living example for my daughter of all the qualities and characteristics I wish for in her. In other words, I needed to walk the talk.

Wanting my daughter to have an example of what it looks like to work hard in a continual pursuit of excellence, I strive to be the best tax lawyer I can be. Wanting my daughter to aspire to her own dream, I allow myself to pursue mine.

THERE IS A PASSAGE in the Stephen Sondheim musical "Into the Woods" that has come to embody this drive for me.

Careful the things you say

Children will listen.

Careful the things you do

Children will see and learn

Children may not obey, but children will listen

Children will look to you for which way to turn

To learn what to be

Careful before you say, Listen to me."

Children will listen.

The idea that my daughter looks to me to learn what to be is a heavy, joyous mantle. The example I had growing up was of a dedicated mother who poured her whole being into raising my siblings and me. It was an excellent example of motherhood. My mother, however, did not pursue a profession. I did not have an example of what it looked like for a woman to have career ambitions, to pursue them, and to be committed to herself and her family.

Simon Sinek, the author of the bestselling book, *Start with Why*, and its companion, *Find Your Why*, once said, "Every single one of us has the opportunity to be the leader we wish we had." More than anything, I want to make sure my daughter has an example of the leader I wish I had: a strong, ambitious, professional woman pursuing her career dreams. So, with a little bit of trepidation, I began to step outside of my self-imposed limitations and into my own value.

REMEMBER THAT DREAM of working on a Supreme Court case? Opportunity presented itself not long after I returned to work from parental leave. My firm received word while I was on leave that the Court granted certiorari to the appeal filed by our opposing counsel on a tax case that was poised to either reinforce or upend 50 years of precedent.

Once the date for argument was set, I remember hemming and hawing over whether I would attend in person. The role I played as part of the team was small so I would not have a place at counsel table. I would not even have a guaranteed spot in the courtroom as a reserved guest. But, heck, it was a real, live Supreme Court appeal that I worked on! It was my dream. I remember saying to my husband I did not want to look back on that opportunity and regret not being there.

I went.

While attending the arguments themselves would be an experience I'll never forget, that was not a part of the trip that will be forever etched into my memory. At the time, my daughter was 6 months old and I was still nursing. There I stood in the line for lawyers admitted to practice before the Court, wearing a pink and purple plaid suit, pumping in public so as not to lose my place in line (go coat cape, Freemie cups, and battery powered pump!). I recall thinking that Ruth (as my daughter calls the late, great Justice) would be tickled pink at the thought of me.

Following the argument, when I no longer needed to reserve a space in line, I decided to hunt down a more private space for another round of pumping. Did you know that the part of the Court open to the public has two viewing rooms playing a video reel about the Court? Ensconced as I was in one of those rooms for another round of pumping—all to myself—I had a moment to reflect. In that moment standing in line, fully embracing my identity as both lawyer and mother, I felt like a badass.

It crystallized my now deeply held conviction that motherhood is a force to be reckoned with in the law. Motherhood has been a catalyst. The desire to have my daughter grow up with an example of a strong confident woman inspired me to project that confidence. It was more than "fake it till you make it." It was a need to truly embody the confidence I want to instill in her.

TRANS ACTIVIST JEFFREY MARSH once asserted, "You are worthy of kindness and respect." Wishing for my daughter to be kind to herself and have self-respect, I embarked on a journey of self-compassion. Self-respect goes hand in hand with self-confidence; the key was recognizing that I am inherently and eminently worthy of both.

I continue to nurture my value (and, in turn, my own success) by surrounding myself with a community of other women—many of them mothers—who inspire me. I learned in my early days of motherhood just how capable I was on my own. Surrounded by support, however, I discovered that ultra-independence no longer served me.

In a community of lawyers who are mothers, I found women whose experiences were similar to my own. I found resources to help me learn to advocate for myself, and the support of thousands of women who encouraged me to do so. In time, advocating for myself morphed into passionate advocacy for other lawyer moms.

The saying goes: "Empowered women empower women." I also experienced a reversal of that sentiment: "Empowering other women empowers me." This has been true in spades in my own life. I find it so fulfilling, so satisfying, to champion others. Although raised more often in the context of beating burnout, many have observed that acting in service of others—specifically in supporting them and championing them—really is empowering.[7] That has been my experience.

Justice Ruth Bader Ginsburg once said, "Fight for the things that you care about, but do it in a way that will lead others to join you." I do not compete with women; I compete for them. I passionately advocate for lawyer moms to be recognized for the tour de force we are, to be embraced on a level playing field, and to be celebrated within the profession. There is more than plenty to go around, and we are all the better for uplifting one another. We will leave a legacy of strength for those coming in our wake—be they daughters or fellow lawyers.

STEPPING INTO MY OWN value with confidence has, in the end, meant opening the door to my own success. Cheesy as it may sound, I tell myself "I am damn good at what I do." (As someone for whom cursing is not natural, my use of "damn" in this way has been very intentional.)

We are the stories we tell to ourselves about ourselves. Success for me has been learning just how big an impact it makes when I ensure that the story I tell myself is a damn strong one. I am writing my story. I am my story. I own my story.

I am Jamie Szal.

First of my name.

Mother of my fierce, little imp.

---

[7] See https://hbr.org/2016/11/beating-burnout; https://www.nytimes.com/2021/04/30/well/workplace-burnout-advice.html; https://knowledge.wharton.upenn.edu/article/why-teams-are-the-key-to-beating-burnout/.

Champion of women.

Sultana of SALT.

Counselor and advocate of businesses.

Community builder.

Writer. Chanteuse. Orator.

I am me.

We write the story. We are the story. We own the story. —Gary Graham, fashion designer

CHAPTER TWENTY-THREE

Reflections of Pride

by Lauren A. Tetenbaum

"With diligence, emotional and other types of intelligence, and some luck, I have achieved a lot. While I admit that I can still feel insecure, I also feel I am a success. Because when I look at me, I see someone who uses authenticity to help others. I see someone who can and does make a difference."

DO YOU LOOK AT ME and see success? You could.

I have everything I used to dream about having, and I am grateful for that. I have my health and a partner and children who love me, a career that is both challenging and flexible, friends who support me, opportunities to contribute to my local and broader communities, and joy from small moments.

After attending an Ivy League university, I earned a master's degree and law degree simultaneously within four years when they'd typically take at least five. On my first try, I passed three states' bar exams. I also became a licensed social worker. I found meaningful work as a post-graduate fellow and again upon moving to a foreign country the following year. Once back in my hometown of New York City, I worked for top law firms as an associate and in personnel roles, earning more with each new opportunity. Following my career pivot during the pandemic, my new business earned a profit within its first two months.

Do you look at me and see failure? You could.

I attended one of my "safety school" law schools, and in some classes, I received my worst grades since ninth grade biology. I was not awarded multiple public-interest post-grad fellowships I'd expected, leaving me without a clear professional plan. I was paid below market rates for my entire legal career. I have been pushed out of what I thought were my dream roles. I have questioned whether I am smart enough to have a career, even though I always wanted one, and whether I am a good enough mother. I have experienced imposter syndrome. Yes, it is real.

WHEN YOU LOOK AT ME, what do you see?

You could look at me as someone with strengths and with flaws, with life experiences that led to nonlinear paths to achieve my goals. You could see me as someone who has felt beaten down by bosses, been talked down to, and told to keep my head down at work because speaking up as a young woman wouldn't look good. You could see me as someone who has maintained high spirits, who has reframed my own narrative, and who has focused on uplifting other young women.

I gained admittance and a merit scholarship to an Ivy League law program but I chose to attend a lower-ranked school for a variety of reasons (and because I lacked awareness of the impact of prestige on earning potential; yet, I do not believe in its justification). Maybe my choice was a poor one, or maybe it was just an opportunity to follow my instincts. The bad grades I mentioned earlier were Bs; but I received As, too.

I graduated during a recession. I started my professional life at a comparatively low salary just to have a job. All the corporate roles I have had since were based off that initial salary, as the law prohibiting asking about salary history had not yet been passed in my state.

What I thought were my ideal jobs were ultimately not ones for which I was willing to compromise my values. There were times I refused to come into the office on a Sunday with a 4-month-old at home after a week of working until midnight, my own work complete; times when I needed to log-in to my kid's Zoom school instead of answering non–time-sensitive emails immediately; and times when I chose to leave the office at certain hours to not only relieve my childcare but also to simply be with my family. There were times when I chose boundaries and personal happiness. I do not regret those choices.

There were times I was told—by other women lawyers—to be quieter, to literally talk less because I didn't have the appropriate pedigree in their eyes, to refrain from asking for what I deserved regarding parental leave and salary because the policies were meant to be accepted as status quo.

NOW, HOW DO YOU SEE ME?

I am and will always be an advocate for myself, for other women, and for others who don't have a voice. I know I am fortunate in many ways and I will loudly speak up when and where I can in order to create positive change. Experiencing imposter syndrome is a struggle I still encounter. To overcome it, I practice self-compassion—one of my favorite therapeutic tools—and I rely on various forms of support.

When I look at me, I see someone I am proud to be.

Ever since I was a child, I have felt compelled to be a resource for women experiencing vulnerability. I grew up in a privileged but socially conscious and feminist household where my father was respectful and loving to all the women in his life. My mother, a naturalized citizen who left her home country with only what she could carry, began her second master's degree when I, the oldest of three, was in high school. I watched her study, work, volunteer, and enjoy her family. I learned from them the way that women should be treated and how much women can accomplish when people believe in them and truly partner with them.

I began my advocacy for women as a teenager, interning for Planned Parenthood headquarters' marketing department, fundraising for the largest social services organization for women in Israel, and serving as my high school's Women's Issues Club president. I went to college to study communications because I thought I'd want to write for women's magazines, connecting people through stories and advice on shared experiences.

I marched for women's lives with Hillary Clinton in Washington, D.C., in 2004. I performed in *The Vagina Monologues*, raising funds for the only rape crisis center in Philadelphia and bringing awareness of sexual assault to many of the fraternities on campus. For my minor in Women's Studies (naturally), I took a course on gender and the law during my sophomore year in college and got hooked on the idea that I could really accomplish something on behalf of women as a lawyer and professional advocate.

I volunteered my junior and senior years at a legal nonprofit so I could learn the basics about divorce law, family law, and domestic violence–based restraining orders. As a telephone counselor, I spoke to people who needed help and resources and just someone to listen to them. I loved it.

I missed working directly with people during my 1L year so I chose to also pursue a master's in Social Work. Throughout graduate school, I interned and volunteered with numerous organizations dedicated to advocating for gender equality and reproductive rights, as well as assisting immigrants and survivors of domestic violence or human trafficking.

In 2011, I became a lawyer.

In 2021, I left the practice of law altogether.

I REMAIN DEDICATED TO helping women personally and professionally, despite no longer working as a lawyer. I have successfully campaigned for more comprehensive parental leave policies at law firms. I have coached women on staying in the workforce by implementing and advocating for more manageable schedules that align with the needs of their full lives. I have brought dozens of isolated moms together for connection when they needed it most, all while raising thousands of dollars for nonprofits helping underserved women and families. I have provided mental health services to depressed teenagers and emerging adults. I have counseled pregnant and postpartum women suffering from anxiety and mentored working parents.

A professional mentor (who happens to be a man and a lawyer) recently remarked about my work since leaving law: "It's amazing how much you've done in such a short period of time. Very inspiring!" But in many ways I've been preparing to do the work I do now throughout my entire life.

While I did, technically, stop being a lawyer on my route to getting here, I unequivocally believe there is a place for women lawyers at law firms and in other companies or settings where men typically dominate. As my favorite woman lawyer, Ruth Bader Ginsburg, said: "Women belong in all places where decisions are being made."

And when I look at my coauthors and beyond, I am the one inspired. I see other women lawyers equally determined to achieve gender equity in our society, to promote opportunities for each other, and to get what we deserve. I see a community. I see advocates for achieving happy lives that include successful careers, knowing that some days are going to be less balanced than others and that having a village (whether or not you have children) is invaluable.

I believe that success, like beauty, is in the eye of the beholder. Upward mobility can be important, but so is the adversity: the zigzag, the road less traveled, the one step forward and two steps backward paths. But hardship builds strength and resilience. It creates an opportunity to make a change—which, at its core, being a lawyer is all about, right?

WHEN YOU LOOK AT yourself, what do you see?

If you don't love what you see, consider adjusting your attitude to one of acceptance, kindness, and appreciation. Take the time to reflect on your priorities, values, and goals. Know that it is okay if they have shifted over time, along with your identity. Think about who you want to be now. Practice empathy.

As I was writing this piece, I received a message from a woman whose children play with mine, a working mother who participated in one of the mom support groups I established and facilitated during the pandemic. She thanked me for providing tips on how to push back on the idea that moms should always be the default parent when it comes to childcare and household management. She called me an inspiring advocate. She made me smile and she made me cry. I don't need her validation to feel that I am doing good; but I do appreciate it.

Though I am not particularly religious, I firmly believe in the Jewish tradition of *tikkun olam*: of taking action via good deeds to pursue social justice and repair the world. As a lawyer, my good deeds have included obtaining orders of protection and visas on behalf of single moms, members of the LGBTQ community, and teenagers who survived various forms of abuse.

I am proud my legal skills and education gave me the opportunities to do so. In this present moment, I am even prouder to be an "inspiring advocate" without needing to be a lawyer. I just need to be myself.

With diligence, emotional and other types of intelligence, and some luck, I have achieved a lot. While I admit that I can still feel insecure, I also feel I am a success. Because when I look at me, I see someone who uses authenticity to help others. I see someone who can and does make a difference.

I see me.

Ms. JD

Your purchase of *Women in Law Discovering the True Meaning of Success* provides much-needed resources to Ms. JD, a nonprofit, nonpartisan organization dedicated to the success of aspiring and early-career women lawyers. Ms. JD is governed by a volunteer board of directors composed of law students and recent graduates and supported by a small group of independent contractors.

Founded at Stanford Law School in 2006 by a group of female law students from Boalt Hall (UC Berkeley), Cornell, Georgetown, Harvard, NYU, Stanford, UCLA, UT Austin, the University of Chicago, the University of Michigan, the University of Virginia, and Yale, Ms. JD is a 501(c)(3) incorporated in California.

Ms. JD seeks to support and improve the experiences of women law students and lawyers. Obstacles to equal participation hinder not only women in the law but also their colleagues, clients, children, and communities. Ms. JD consequently strives to give voice to why it matters that women continue to overcome barriers to achieve gender parity in the profession. In doing so, Ms. JD spreads the word: *Women's victories are everyone's victories.*

Serving as a unique nexus between the profession and the pipeline of diverse attorneys, Ms. JD's online community provides a forum for dialogue and networking among women lawyers and law students. With campus chapters throughout the nation, Ms. JD is also home to the National Women Law Students' Organization.

Ms. JD celebrates women's achievements, addresses remaining challenges, and facilitates continued progress by bringing legal practitioners and law students together to share in an ongoing conversation about gender issues in law school and the profession.

Visit https://ms-jd.org/.